A Memory Returned

A Memory Returned

Healing in its Deepest Form

Second Edition

By **Anna Delves**
Author of 'From Chrysalis to Butterfly'

AuthorHouse™
1663 Liberty Drive
Bloomington, IN 47403
www.authorhouse.com
Phone: 1-800-839-8640

Published by AuthorHouse 04/20/2013

ISBN: 978-1-4678-7945-3 (sc)
ISBN: 978-1-4678-7946-0 (e)

This book is printed on acid-free paper.

To lose a son is devastating, but to receive such deep revelations from him from the 'other' side was mind blowing.

He and I invite you to learn and grow as you read this book.

Contents

Acknowledgements

There are certain people to whom I am deeply indebted and without whom this book could not have been completed.

The first is my eldest son, Dom. His gift to us, from where he is, is invaluable and I thank him on behalf of us all, for his honesty and dedication to duty, from the bottom of my heart.

I have a few other family members to whom I am greatly indebted: my sister, Fiona, who has tirelessly helped me in so many ways to produce all my books; my husband, Rod, who, among other things, looked after the farm while I was in Peru; my younger son, Charles Edward, who has sorted out my naughty computer on numerous occasions; my mum, Peggy, who never ceases to run the farm and the retreat so efficiently from her lofty position on the other side; and, finally, my dogs, Tassle and Derby, who have put up with me through thick and thin.

Enormous thanks go to Ingrid, who accompanied me to Peru. Her selfless efforts were hugely valuable in bringing the truth through.

And how can I thank all my guests and friends adequately? Without you, I could not have learnt all that I have learnt over the last few years. Whether it was in the sharing of your personal experiences or the questions you asked, all of it has helped to complete and enrich this story.

A Note from the Author

I have been a channel for healing for as long as I can remember. My training has come direct form the source of all that is and has been intense, soul-searching and yet very rewarding. I continue to grow every day, as I yearn to understand in greater and greater detail, just what 'we' are all about. My learning enhances all that I do to help people and takes me ever closer towards enlightenment.

My sole purpose in life is to 'serve'. I have fun 'serving' but always remain true to who I am. The more I help people, the happier I become, living confidently in the knowledge that we are increasing the light on the planet every day.

I live on a beautiful farm in the Cotswolds, 110 acres in size—replete with sheep, honey bees, two dogs and a couple of Dartmoor ponies—which I currently open as a retreat during the summer months. People from all over the world come and enjoy the seclusion, tranquillity and peace that embrace the farm at all times. All guests receive healing and unconditional love while staying, either from myself, the farm itself or other guests. The farm definitely catapults those who are searching for their deepest truths into an acceleration process which is most beneficial, taking them on their journey with increased speed.

My youngest son, Charles Edward (known as Edward), currently lives on the farm with me, which I find a great joy and support. My daughter, Jo, lives nearby in Cirencester and is learning her life's lessons in the best place for her. She visits me regularly. We are a very close family and the guests who visit are embraced in this 'family' as equals.

If you wish to visit or simply to discuss any aspect of this book, or if you think I might be able to help you in any way, please contact me through my website: www.cotswoldhealingretreat.co.uk

Foreword

In the beginning was light, and the light was in darkness, and the darkness comprehended it not.

All that existed was 'light' or nothingness. And yet, because of the light, darkness existed, darkness being the opposite of light and being the word used here to depict 'that which the light didn't know'. And so it came to pass that the two grew together, in equal measure.

Right from the beginning, light grew through the universe from the source, feeling its way along the journey, spreading gently through the universal system, knowing its contact with the source and feeling the constant need to 'push forward' into the unknown.

It met planets on its way and integrated with their masses, bringing light into their systems in various ways. Each planet brought its own 'teaching', allowing the light more knowledge of itself as it 'experienced' itself each time.

Much of the following writings were received from my beloved eldest son, Dom, who left this life on 2 July 2008. I gift these revelations to you, in order that you may understand as much as you can, thus helping to release your own unique 'light' back into our planet.

Introduction

Dom was born on 19 January 1981. He was a very poorly baby, spending many weeks in Great Ormond Street Hospital. He was allergic to many foods until he was 4 years old when he received a wonderful healing (as described fully in *From Chrysalis to Butterfly*, 2008) and from then on was always in good health. He was very active and independent as a child and extremely good looking to boot, with white/ blond hair and blue eyes.

From the age of 8 to about 12/13, he was bullied at school and never really had any friends. Dom's love of tennis kept him happy, though he could also have been a county cricketer or county/national runner if he had wanted. He started to make friends properly at about the age of 15 and from then on he never looked back. At his funeral, I realised just how many close friends he had, and I think it was because he really took time to be with them, contact them regularly and was very good to them. I sensed that Dom was much happier as an adult than he had ever been as a child.

He had a wonderful three years of university life in Liverpool, studying law and being part of the marine corps.

He was also a Wimbledon umpire through those years and achieved quite a high qualification before his career in the forces took over. 'I want to do good in the world', he said of joining the Royal Marines. Right from his school days (when he never succumbed to the pressures of smoking) and beyond, he was never afraid to stand up and be counted for what he believed in.

Dom and I were incredibly close and he always told everyone how much he loved his mum (I found this out after he died). He would come to me in times of need and often for healing and advice. His trust of me was second to none. We went on holiday together and loved doing all sorts of things together. I think all of this set the stage for what has happened since he died.

As he lay dying in June 2008, I bravely asked the universe if I could learn and grow as much as possible from the experience.

'Show me healing in its deepest form?' I prayed, little knowing what I was really asking.

This moment proved to be the start of a journey that would take three and a half years to complete and be of enormous planetary significance.

After my son died, I was told I would receive a gift. When he started to transmit revelations that clearly and simply explained how our planet had evolved, I knew I was receiving that gift. I was bowled over that I should be entrusted with such deep and amazing knowledge. I had never really delved into the source of our creation before, always being more concerned with the here and now. The revelations came as a complete surprise to me. I did not know I was being prepared for a very important job that would later help alter and heal the balance of our planet in such a profound way.

After receiving the first few revelations, I began sharing my new-found knowledge with appropriate guests coming to the retreat, learning, at the same time, how to communicate it, when to communicate it and which parts to communicate. It was completely exhausting for me to continually repeat and explain all that I knew and it often took several hearings before my listeners actually grasped enough of what I was trying to convey, to allow them to truly benefit.

The Butterfly Spreads its Wings was my first attempt to put everything of this into words. However, the world as we know it is changing so rapidly that one year later I had to rewrite the book incorporating all the extra knowledge I received throughout 2011, culminating in my extraordinary experiences in Peru during the October of that year. I could not have foreseen how important my trip to Peru was to be. In fact, I'm glad I didn't or I wouldn't have been able to do what I had to do, with such ease and clarity. But the journey is now done. It is ready to be shared with everyone. This book is a complete work at last and will bring massive insight and understanding to those who are interested in what our planet is currently going through.

On a more personal level, if you are choosing to heal in the deepest possible way, these writings will help you along your path. My sincerest wish, while completing this work, was to be as accurate as possible, thus bringing as much enlightenment to you all as I could. Enlightenment begins with you. As you become enlightened, so you enlighten all that is around you . . . and thus you enlighten the world.

It has been very difficult to put these insights into word form, especially in Chapter 7. I trust this book will do its job in the highest possible way.

Ask to learn all that you can as you read and you will benefit to the maximum.

Jesus once said, 'It is easier for a camel to pass through the eye of a needle than for a rich man to enter the kingdom of God'. The following revelations help us understand just what Jesus meant and how we ourselves can pass through the 'eye of the needle' that he was talking about. It doesn't happen overnight. We have to be aware of the eye before we can start to move through it. Some people think they can take their *baggage* through. They try every which way to do so. But, of course, in the end they realise that it just won't go. The only way through the eye is to strip ourselves of all that we (think) we are and give ourselves fully into service. Then, and only then, can we slide back through to the place where wisdom, love, peace and joy reside within us in perfect harmony.

'Then all these gifts will be added unto you . . . Alleluia.'

1

Balance Explained

Dom enjoyed rock climbing. In August 2008, he was due to embark on a mountains leaders' course as part of his training with the Royal Marines. He had already begun the course the previous year, but after only one month's training he had tripped on rough ground and broken his arm. Therefore, he had been forced to delay the course for 11 months. He decided to have another attempt because the qualifications it would give him would allow him to train other marines to climb and could also be of use in a future civilian career.

In the late spring, Dom decided to go and do some practice climbs, trying to get himself back into the swing of climbing before the new course began. He took off one sunny Sunday, accompanied by his younger brother, Edward and his girlfriend, Eileen. He chose a very picturesque spot, near the Devon coast, six miles from Plymouth. After deliberating on the best place to ascend, he began his climb and reached his first destination safely, a ledge about 65 metres above the ground. But as he started to abseil back down to ground level, something happened and he fell. He landed on extremely rocky terrain, crashing his head on some sharp rocks and falling very quickly unconscious.

He survived in hospital for 10 days, but did not regain consciousness before he died. The following is an account of what happened between my son and I during his last 10 days.

When I entered the intensive care unit where Dom was lying, a few hours after his accident, I realised immediately that he wasn't in his body. His body was lying on a bed, heavily drugged to stop him moving, so I said to the Dom I could feel floating swiftly up and down the room: 'Dom, this is your body. It isn't a joke. You are actually looking at your own body. Go back in and see for yourself.' I felt him stop abruptly in his tracks and a massive shock run through him. I heard his thoughts: 'Oh no, that can't be right.' So I said, 'Yes, Dom. Go back in your body and have a look at the truth for yourself'. I felt him slide back into his body. After a short while, I left the room, to give him time to come to terms with the situation.

The next time I visited Dom, he was safely back in his body and was taking on full recognition of what had happened. I knew I could not communicate with him at this point so I decided to leave him until he was ready to contact me.

Sometime later—I forget which part of the hospital I was in—I felt Dom around me again. He wanted to discuss everything with me, which was quite natural to him when he was in trouble. He knew I could hear him because we had already communicated. We discussed the damage to his brain and the general physical state of his body. We discussed whether he could pull his body back from this situation in a way that would enable him to live a future life with some sort of meaning. Having talked over every aspect, he then went off to consider it all and to see how he could go about healing himself.

Meanwhile, his girlfriend Eileen and I were offering his body healing, the doctors were keeping him stable with drugs and all that could be done to give him the best chance of recovery, including further operations, was being done.

Over the next few days, I made it clear to Dom that he would only receive full healing if he truthfully faced himself, faults and all. We discussed, in detail, the main issues that troubled him in this life and he managed to face them all full on and accept them for what they were. He accepted he had not handled them correctly and promised never to run away from them again. We faced character difficulties he had and how he could put them right. These things were not achieved quickly. It took a lot of trust on his part and a lot of admission. But it was not a new process. Dom and I had done many mini sessions like this in the past, but never before at such a deep level and with such intense sincerity. Dom knew he had to lay himself completely bare if he was to have any chance of survival.

By the time the doctors decided to try and bring Dom round, he felt ready to attempt a return to life. Over the next day or so, his physical condition swung back and forth precariously and, eventually, due to an infection, the doctors had to fully sedate him again.

I found myself back in communication with Dom. We discussed the possibility of him giving his life totally into the service of God. This might mean he could carry on as a Royal Marine . . . but it might not. It might mean that he could live at his beloved farm again one day . . . but it might not. It might mean he could keep his current girlfriend . . . but it might not. But giving his life to God and relinquishing all his earthly desires would mean that the highest good for humanity would be achieved, and Dom decided that whatever the cost to himself, this was what he wanted.

A little while later, when I was sitting at Dom's bedside, I said to the nurse, 'It would take a miracle to help him now, wouldn't it?' She nodded slowly. As I sat there, I prayed as I had never prayed before. I asked God to show me *healing in its deepest form*. After a while, I felt healing energy circulating in the quietness of the room. I felt it surround Dom and I felt its power.

A little later, I went upstairs to the hospital chapel. As I entered, the atmosphere inside was overwhelmingly powerful. I can only attempt to describe it as thick, almost tangible, and as I walked further into the chapel I felt I might faint at any moment. I looked up at the plain wooden cross above the altar and became aware that, in that very moment, Dom was giving his life to God in an 'unconditional' way. I plonked myself unsteadily onto a chair in front of the cross and felt the tears streaming down my face. I felt so incredibly proud of Dom. It was a moment like no other. I sat in silence and shared his private experience in awe. No one came in to disturb us.

I don't know how long I sat in the chapel for but, after a while, I felt the atmosphere clear a little and I managed to get up shakily and make my way back downstairs to Dom's unit. My emotions were swinging like billio at this point. Sometimes I felt Dom was definitely going to live and sometimes I felt his body was too damaged and he was gone. But, at all times, I continued to pray for the highest good to happen, whatever it might be.

Shortly after this, the doctors told us they had controlled the infection in Dom's body and had decided to have another go at pulling him back into consciousness. I connected with Dom and felt he was willing to give life another go. As I felt him slipping back into his body, I left him to it.

But the battle to heal his body had become too great by this time. A lot of his vital organs had started packing up and I think Dom realised he was too damaged to have any decent future quality of life. After a further 24 hours, the doctors suggested turning the ventilators off and Dom died peacefully an hour later.

I knew that the process Dom and I had been through while he was lying unconscious had completed most of the life objectives he had pre-set for this life. The content of our discussions had accelerated his progress so much that he had died quite spiritually grown. I felt terrific joy for him in that, because we had achieved the 'greater plan' if not the human desire!

The day after Dom's funeral, I was lying outside in a long chair and must have momentarily dropped off to sleep. I remember dreaming I was squatting on the edge of a small ledge with my face to the rock face and my back to the elements. I then felt my feet slip, first the left one and then the right, very specifically in that order. I thought I was falling and I woke up with a huge start. I immediately knew Dom had been trying to show me how he fell. I rushed into the kitchen where Eileen was busy cooking and asked her what position she had last seen Dom in when he had been on the ledge. She said, 'Squatting'. So I had my confirmation. I was only later to realise how important this little incident was.

I had the overwhelming feeling that it had not been on Dom's blueprint that he was to die at this time. I suppose I kept asking the question, 'Why? Why did it happen?' I felt a desperate need to know why I had lost the son I had never suspected I would lose. I had been told these were my last children many years ago and that I would be able to enjoy them to the full. What had happened? What had changed and how could it? My mind never stopped. Many people visiting the retreat had ideas about it and told me it was his time to go. I didn't believe them. It simply didn't feel right to me.

Some nine months later, Dom's girlfriend, Eileen, came to stay with me the night before the inquest. She reluctantly showed me the last picture she had ever taken of Dom. It was taken 20 minutes before he died. She didn't like it and she wasn't sure why. I took one look at the photo and I was flabbergasted. It showed a picture of Dom and Eileen close together. The energy around Eileen looked vibrant and alive. The energy around Dom looked dark and closed. It was horribly apparent and when I pointed it out to Eileen she knew immediately what I meant. I said to her, 'He had already gone!'

We both then knew that, at that point in time, his death was already known, at some level. The picture did not look like Dom at all. I felt I never wanted to see it again.

The day of the inquest dawned and little did I know what an astonishing day it would prove to be. We arrived in Plymouth to find the Royal Marines parading around the town, having just come back from a tour in Afghanistan. As we approached the courtroom in the centre of the town, the Marines seemed to be everywhere, playing their band music and marching in long columns with crowds lining the streets, clapping and cheering. It was nothing to do with us, of course, but at the same time it felt like it was everything to do with us.

There was a Royal Marine mountain expert at the inquest who was drafted in by the court to give his opinion on how the accident happened. My younger son, Edward and Dom's girlfriend, Eileen had to give evidence as to what they had witnessed on the day. It was to be the first full account of the accident the rest of the family had ever heard.

transpired that the Royal Marine expert, from ... evidence showing on the ground at the scene of the accident, thought Dom had safely climbed up the rock face, being belayed by Edward. When he reached the top, he put his two anchor points in, ran the rope between the anchor points and tied a knot. At this point, he called to Edward that he was safe.

He busied himself up on the ledge for a while and the expert explained that, at that stage, Dom would have probably realised he couldn't abseil down because of the knot, so he would have tried to undo it. He said that it looked as if Dom had slipped at that point—the anchor points had failed to hold him and he had fallen. Both anchor points were found on the ground. It was evident to the Royal Marine expert that Dom had not put his anchor points in with a 50-50 weighting. He had put them in unevenly, which was why they had not held his weight and saved his life. A verdict of accidental death was given.

After the inquest, we, the family, decided to go and visit the spot where Dom had fallen. We climbed over very rough terrain to the scene of the accident. I looked at the sharp rocks at the foot of the cliff, wondering which one had dealt the fatal blow. Then I looked up at the ledge from which Dom had fallen and, to my amazement, I could see him waving and smiling down at me from the top. He spoke clearly: 'This is the last thing I remember, mum. I don't remember being on the ground.' These were very comforting words for a troubled and grieving mum! He also let me know he had been extremely happy in his last moments.

I looked up again at the ledge to which Dom had climbed. I could just make out where his anchor points would have been. I suddenly realised there was no way that Dom could have fallen from that ledge. There was a tree growing out from the centre and it would have caught him or at least made quite a noise of breaking branches as he fell past it, which neither his brother nor Eileen had heard. My glance slid to a foot below the ledge where there was a long crack in the rock running almost parallel to the ledge but on a distinct slant. The slant ran across the rock face, the left side lower than the right.

My brain started to turn crazy somersaults. It became abundantly clear to me that Dom had started to abseil down the cliff face, realised the knot was stopping him, and put his feet in the convenient crack to take his weight and balance himself while he tried to undo the knot. Of course, the exact angle of the crack would mean that most of his weight would have been on his left foot! My brain tracked back to the dream I had had the day after the funeral. So that was why I had felt my left foot slide first and the right foot afterwards! My gaze was riveted on the crack in my sudden comprehension.

My mind moved on . . . The anchor points that should have held him were not placed in a balanced way and therefore did not hold him when his weight suddenly required it. I felt incredibly sick. I knew I had come as close as anyone could, to knowing what had happened and why. Dom had given me such a distinct clue in the dream, the day after the funeral. And the anchor points were a *huge* sign that Dom was not balanced in his life. The opinion of the Royal Marine expert was given as a confirmation of this fact.

Hence, it was with utter dismay that I suddenly realised Dom had been functioning from a very vulnerable position. The tough life tests he had experienced during the last two years had pushed him beyond a level he could cope with. Therefore, he had been living on the vulnerable side of his pivot point for the last few months but none of us had known it. I knew, of course, that he was being pushed very, very hard but I thought I would be able to help him gently over the coming years. I did not understand that once we are functioning on the vulnerable side of our pivot point, our survival is dependent on the will of the collective consciousness.

If you are wondering what a decent young man like Dom could have been doing to become so vulnerable, I will explain:

Two years previously, Dom had had a short friendship with a young lady of a similar age to himself. It was nothing serious, he just took her out occasionally. She had previously been married and she told Dom that she couldn't have children. He, being a very trusting sort, believed her and took a silly risk by having unprotected sex. It didn't take Dom too long before he realised she was not the one for him and he told her he didn't want to take her out any more. Shortly afterwards, he left for a tour in Afghanistan feeling he was free to go his own way and so was she.

Little did he know that she was already pregnant. I will not go into any detail about what happened between them except to say that the situation being as it was, and my naive son being such a sensitive and trusting soul, the ensuing financial battle blew his mind into a terrible place.

Although I was very upset for my son, like any mother would be, I thought I had plenty of time to help Dom accept the consequences of his former 'silly' actions. I thought I could one day help him accept that the baby was his and that he had a responsibility towards his son. I was convinced that if I could persuade the young lady to leave Dom alone for a while, he would calm down and I could help them both to see the situation in a more reasonable light. I had written to her explaining this but had not had a reply.

At this time, Dom was coming home nearly every weekend. I knew it was because he needed refuge from what was going on and I didn't question him, feeling his home should rightly be the refuge he sought. However, he was obviously very bitter and was saying some pretty harsh things. He didn't mean them, of course, but he was at the time receiving phone calls during the night, and when he picked up the phone he could hear the baby screaming on the other end of the line. He was also experiencing the mother hounding him at his flat on a regular basis. The more she hounded him, the angrier he became. He wouldn't willingly talk about it to any of us in the family. He was shutting us, and the situation, out.

Around the end of April that same year (about two months before Dom had his accident), I had felt an energetic change around the farm. I had also been told by the universe that my deceased mother had to go and do another job (in the spirit world) and I was informed I would have a temporary guide. This temporary guide turned out to be a novice and I thought, at the time, that I was being used to give her an opportunity to work with someone like me.

Everything in my diary began to empty. I had just opened the retreat and was starting to take bookings. Suddenly no more bookings came in. I just had a few enquiries that came to nothing. My own personal diary became empty. I found myself wandering around the farm saying to the universe, 'Well, OK. I'm here if you need me but I accept it if you don't.' I was beginning to think I wasn't going to run a retreat after all! However, that seemed very strange, after all the work and finance that had gone into it. There was a kind of hush around me, and I didn't know why.

On 22 June 2008, Dom fell. It was immediately apparent to me why my life had come to a standstill. It was also immediately apparent that the universe had known from the end of April that Dom's time was near. He had, at that moment, crossed the fatal line; he was on the wrong side of his pivot point. He was vulnerable! My mother had withdrawn from me in order to prepare, as much as she could, for the oncoming event.

From 22 June until 2 July when he died, Dom was in the hands of the collective consciousness. He was given time with me to come to terms with his situation which is exactly what he did. He was given the time to face himself and fulfil his life purpose before he died. At the moment he gave his life to God, he was once more finely balanced. If it had been in the highest interests of the collective consciousness that he should make a full recovery, then that is what would have happened. If it had been in the highest interests that he should make a partial recovery, it would have impacted on his entire family in a different way, but that is what would have happened. But it was in the highest interests of the collective consciousness that he should die, so that is what did happen.

We, as mere mortals, can never know what the 'highest' good for the collective consciousness can be. We cannot judge. We cannot see the bigger picture. But we can be aware of the highest good for ourselves, when we are balanced and centred.

The greatest message Dom has brought us from the other side is to let us know what happened to him and why. Through the anchor points, he brought us factual proof, for if he had been 'balanced' he would have weighted his anchor points evenly. There is a tipping point for each of us, all of the time, and we can all become vulnerable if we don't redress the balance. Once in the hands of the collective consciousness, we still have the chance to redress it in this life, unless we die first. You might ask why murderers live on for so many years after they have committed such an awful crime. That is a question I have asked! But, of course, the answer to serving in the highest way is not ours to know. The facts surrounding the murderer are not weighable by humans but they are weighed carefully by our spiritual counterparts and the best result allowed.

I did ask Dom why so many people came to the farm and told me it was his time to go. He said, 'We had to allow it, mum. We had to make you question!' He also confirmed to me that it had not been on his blueprint that he should die at this point and he has never ceased to apologise and to help me in every way he can. I do not ask this of him. He chooses to do this.

While I still miss my son very, very much, the peace that I have over his death is complete at every level. We now work together to bring this and other knowledge to those who are ready to hear. One of the other gifts it has brought is my fuller understanding of our total life path from source to the present day, and how the knowledge of where we were at the time of the Split is so crucial to healing our current emotions.

This planet has always been about 'holding the balance' and I was now learning how crucial balance is in every single aspect of creation. Everything has its own balance or pivot point. The world is finely balanced on its axis, trees are finely balanced by their branches, finances are finely balanced though they have recently been swinging about precariously, and honesty is a fine balance that we tread in every walk of life. I could go on and on . . .

The opposites that were created at the time of the Split require us to keep both sides in our sights. When one side heavily outweighs the other, it can be said we are in a vulnerable position. Take the weather, for example. If all the rain falls in one place, it creates destruction on a massive scale. If no rain falls, it can create a famine. When the planet is relatively balanced, the weather takes on a more balanced role and we have a mix of rain and sun. Then everything flourishes. This 'weather' balance can occur on a world-wide scale, a country-size scale or simply a 'one town' scale, as witnessed recently all over the world.

2

The First Set of Revelations

I was walking my dogs one sunny afternoon in early January 2009, something I do every day, when I suddenly became aware that my son, Dom, was walking beside me. This was not too unusual an event, but when it happens I always feel overjoyed and so thankful that I can feel his presence. As we walked along on that particular day, in calm companionship, I suddenly felt him move all around me. It felt as if his energy was encompassing my whole body and giving me a huge hug. I was delighted!

As we progressed along the woodland path, I felt as if spirit and incarnated soul had become one. It felt as if my son and I were one. It was fabulous. I gradually became aware that my consciousness was no longer solely confined to my body but had expanded into quite a big area outside my body. I therefore felt as if I was walking among and through the trees that surrounded me and that I was far, far bigger than my physical self. I began to communicate with the trees and the other parts of nature I was passing. I heard the trees telling me their history; about how they communicated with each other, how they touched each other and how they were aware of each other in differing ways. I passed one tree valiantly holding up another tree and I said to it: 'Why are you doing this? Your friend has nearly died and needs to fall. You are wasting your energy and also preventing your friend from moving on into spirit.' I felt the tree's shocked surprise and left it to ponder!

I started to communicate telepathically with my dogs, Tassle, a border collie and Darby, a black and tan Jack Russell. I managed to achieve the feat of getting Tassle to come and stand at my feet without using my voice. She had previously been running around the wood like a mad thing. I was so excited! In fact, I was ecstatic! I felt the trappings of my earthly body had been hugely removed. This is what I had wanted for so long but had always thought I would have to wait until I died before it would be possible.

After a while, the woodland path started to wind up a hill and, as I trudged slowly upwards with my consciousness still expanding, I started to think about energy and where it came from. What exactly was taking my body up the hill? What was gravity? What *was* energy? What was propelling my body forwards?

The next moment, I became aware of my consciousness sliding down a huge dark tube and the tube was going *within.* It felt very strange. Finally, my slide came to a stop and I knew I was at the centre of the earth. I was light (energy) and everything around me was extremely black. I heard a deep booming voice, not my son's, say:

'What you are about to learn now relates to this planet and this planet only.'

I thought a surprised 'OK' and wondered what was going to happen next. From my new perspective at the very core of the earth, I felt the shocked emotions that came from the light energy as it wriggled and squirmed around in itself in its enforced prison. I felt the 'trap' that the light was experiencing and I knew its frustration, anger and fear as it sought to find out what had happened. It seemed as if the resulting emotions went into some sort of fight with each other. Everything felt dark and swirly and I knew light energy was desperately searching for its lost 'freedom'. As the emotions fought, they started to move and as they moved they started to expand. I didn't know it at the time but I know now that this momentous occasion was the first moment on *this* planet that we (light energy) panicked and became full of fear, because we thought we had become separated from source. It was an illusion of course. We were the source . . . But the entrapment in the apparent dark space caused the light energy to feel a type of separation and, as it expanded further and further into the mass that was the earth, the separation 'seemed' more and more real.

I felt this process go on for a while and then felt quite in awe as I started to see the strata of the earth forming. The emotional upheaval was causing a pushing and shoving motion in all directions. I saw the light paths criss-crossing each other as the light energy attempted to know what it was. I felt the emotional struggle in the earth's core getting more and more powerful as the process continued. There were different earth patterns forming everywhere. Some of the light swirled in circles around the core, some seemed to shoot outwards towards the earth's crust in a fairly straight line, and some wriggled its way about, weaving in and around whatever it encountered. There was no set pattern. It was a dynamic, vibrant energy on the move.

Inch by inch, the light shifted outwards from the core. When eventually the light energy grew large enough to reach the earth's crust, I felt a dramatic emotional change as the resistance it encountered altered. There was a long moment of calm, as if the whole planet was drawing in its breath and then suddenly wild eruptions broke out all over the planet's surface. The frustrated, trapped emotions from within were hastening to the freedom they sensed might possibly be without. I experienced massive volcanoes as the light energy tried to escape from its 'apparent' prison. Bottled emotions from the core exploded onto the earth's surface in varying formats, causing earthquakes both under the oceans and on dry land.

In other words, I experienced the most incredible exploding of the mass that we call earth.

I remained connected to this explosive environment for quite a while, sensing the rush, sensing the light energy's search for freedom and knowledge. Words cannot fully express the enormity of this experience.

I realised the light strands that were appearing all over the planet had each taken their own, completely unique, routes to the surface. All these light routes that were criss-crossing each other and erupting in millions of different ways, were our own personal life journeys that we are currently striving to remember and heal. I therefore understood immediately why we all feel we have met each other over and over again and it started from the moment the light energy entered this planet. Our 'knowing' of each other began at the moment we started the process of separation.

Gradually, I suppose over millions of earth years, I felt the planet begin to calm. The eruptions became less severe and the earth as a whole showed signs of lessening turmoil . . .

At this point, my son fast-forwarded my consciousness to a much calmer phase in planetary evolution, where I felt the light energy trying to poke out through the earth's crust. I can only describe it as a distinctly prickly sensation that I felt all over the planet's surface.

The first 'pokers' came out as grasses; tiny shoots that lasted for a millionth of a second and then disappeared. This was the beginnings of what we now call the 'life cycle'. The light *wanted* to experience the air and water outside the confines of the mass and, above all, it yearned for the freedom it sensed might be there . . . so it kept on poking. Gradually, grass learnt to tolerate the new environment for longer and longer periods. Life cycles changed constantly as it did so. Light energy started to spend time incarnate and then return to spend time in spirit again. When it was in spirit, it hugged the earth's surface closely, not wanting to lose the opportunity of reincarnating when it could. I lived the process closely and knew that the grasses all over the planet were emerging in many different guises, depending on the route they had taken from the source and the climate they hit outside. The light energy was being continuously emotionally driven, thus it strained to exist beyond the earth's surface, gradually forming as different varieties of our 'nature'.

My son then once again fast-forwarded the 'slide show' and showed me a lone tree. I knew I was now re-experiencing the time when the trees were the kings of creation. Trees had gradually learnt to outlive the grass's short life cycle and survive for a number of years. Dom showed me a tree communicating with its near neighbours by brushing the branches together as the wind blew. He showed me the baby trees that were growing up quietly at their parent's base, producing the first family units. Trees appeared to have a knowledge and power beyond other evolving species.

As I felt the light energy from the core of the earth continuing its relentless push for knowledge and freedom, there came a moment when I sensed the tree beaming its internal radar over its immediate horizon and becoming aware of other trees in the distance. These were trees it had no communication with. They were too far away.

But it *wanted* communication. I felt such a yearning, such a massive desire to communicate, coming from the tree that eventually it started to create worm-like or maggot-like creatures from within its trunk. They were tiny, bloodless creatures that appeared in their masses, moving constantly over and around each other, slowly and silently. I felt them gradually move 'as one' down the inside of the trunk and then start spilling out from the base of the tree. Their instinct then drove them to begin making their way towards the other trees.

As they felt the 'push' to make the journey from one tree to another (or from one place to another), the maggots mistakenly felt they were undergoing a much greater 'separation' from the light/source. Those first maggots did not survive for very long. A sort of panic ensued! They felt too separated from source to make the journey. The trees still felt connected because they were rooted into the ground. The worms/maggots felt an immense sense of disconnection as they tried to leave the tree, moving in a way that appeared to them to be 'alone'. So the grasses and other vegetation on the path between the trees started calling to the worms/maggots: 'Eat us. Feed off us! Absorb our nutrients'. They saw it as a way for the 'would-be' journeyers to stay connected to the source and therefore have the energy/ability to survive the apparent 'disconnected' distance. Thus, the first form of eating began; the first form of this type of dependence upon each other and the first part of the illusion that we, in animal or human form, need to eat/absorb each other to survive.

Dom then took me through a fairly quick process, enabling me to experience the gradual formation of many other underground animals, followed by over-ground/underground animals and finally totally over-ground animals, developing after thousands, possibly millions, of years into humans. As creatures developed, the eating process developed, all in the name of survival. They all believed that by sustaining one another in this way, the un-rooted would somehow remain fed by the rooted. And once this idea allowed for the survival of the un-rooted, it grew unhindered among all detached creation, in order that they might continue to evolve. So larger animals began to eat smaller animals and humans began to eat them all.

For a fleeting second at this point, the rolling ball of evolution I was experiencing went rapidly on into the future and I became aware that the probability of some type of 'flying' was more than likely.

At about this moment, I partly came out of the very deep trance state I had been in and became aware of my surroundings a little more. Glancing downwards, I realised I was walking up a small, grassy track. The sun was out and while I enjoyed its warmth on my back I noticed the clear, blue sky above. I felt the soft grass beneath my feet and started to apologise to it that I was walking on it and hurting it. This was not the first time in my life this thought had crossed my mind, for I have often wondered if we hurt the grass when we walk on it, but realised we couldn't avoid it, so dismissed it again.

However, as I had the thought this time, the sudden realisation came that I had *been* the grass I was walking on, I had *been* the animals that have eaten the grass, and I had *been* the grass that the animals have eaten. I've been the human who has eaten the animals. I've been the human who the animals have eaten. I am currently the human who eats the grass and the animals. I felt the grass communicating that it was proud to allow me to walk on it because I was part of the most evolved species of creation. The grass wanted to support me as I walked my path, because what I discovered, I discovered for it too. I felt the support system throughout the whole of creation as I had never felt it before, and also a complete unity among incarnated existence.

Stepping out further along the track, I started to realise consciously the enormity and clarity of the revelations I had just received. I marvelled at the whole thing and while still feeling somewhat overwhelmed, I experienced deep, deep gratitude to Dom for giving me such amazing awareness.

The track I was following came out onto a road, which I crossed, and then took a path which led across some fields towards my home. As I crossed the hedged boundary onto my own farmland, I found myself slipping back into a trance state again. I felt the universe communicating to me that the farm was now subject to an advanced set of rules and regulations! I was given to understand that the farm had now come 'consciously' under the direct control of the universe. This meant it would be a completely safe place for anyone or anything to exist, providing we or it 'towed the line'. For example, if the squirrels ate all the bark off the trees and killed them, they might well find that they themselves would later be run over or shot. If they respected the trees, they would find that the trees and the farm would house them perfectly safely. I myself was another example—or indeed any other human on the property. As long as I continued to work for the highest good of all creation, I would be nourished and looked after and kept safe on the farm. If I transgressed, I would receive the punishment due. If the deer ate plants they were not supposed to eat, they might find themselves in trouble, but if they kept to the places they were entitled to graze, they would be quite safe.

These rules would apply to anyone or anything on the farm, regardless of their status. I also knew I would have nothing whatsoever to do with the implementing of these rules; it would all be controlled by the great universal law. I felt quite over-awed by these huge revelations.

As I walked on, I became aware of a strong, golden light coming from the centre of the earth, from the source of all that is, quietly enveloping the whole farm and rising high into the sky above me. I felt it was pure, powerful and healing, and of other qualities way beyond my comprehension. I continued my homeward journey in a state of wonder. What had happened today? Just what had happened today?

As if to confirm these revelations, I was in my yard a few days later when I saw a barn owl sitting on a low branch of an apple tree. This was a very unusual sight for the middle of the day so I stopped and stared at it, feeling very privileged to have such a good view. It sat on the branch so motionlessly that I half suspected it was a wooden owl. However, a minute or so later, it flew off and perched in a nearby cherry tree. I walked towards it as the cherry tree stood right beside the path I wanted to go up. I stopped about three feet away from the branch it was sitting on and stared up at it. It was not much more than 18 inches above my head. Again, I felt it was such a privilege. Eventually, I thought, 'Well, I must go up this path and feed my hens'.

I stepped forward, fully believing that the owl would take off as soon as I moved. It did nothing of the sort! It turned its head and watched me walk right under it. I stared up at it and it stared down at me and clearly told me with its huge round trusting eyes that it knew it was safe.

It took me many, many weeks to stop talking about this wonderful owl incident, because nothing like this had ever happened to me before and it really did confirm that everything I had experienced was true.

Over the next few weeks, I pondered over the enormity of what I had been shown. My understanding of all the revelations expanded as I tried to repeat them to a few people and they were all equally thrilled by the simplicity of what I had been shown.

Not long after the owl incident, two middle-aged ladies I had met only a couple of times before went for a walk around the perimeter of the farm. One of them rang me up and told me of this and asked why the fields on the far side of my boundary had such a horrible energy. I was amazed and said there had *never* been a horrible energy there—it had always been wonderful. She was adamant and said, 'No, it was strongly apparent'.

Both she and her friend had felt this unhappy energy on the other side of my boundary but when they looked across at my farm they had sensed an incredibly pure energy emanating from it. The distinction was extraordinary to them. She asked what I had done!

In an instant, I pictured the scene where I had been walking across my fields on the day of the revelations and I remembered feeling the universe telling me about the powerful golden light. I remembered I had pictured the golden light spreading to the very edge of all my farm boundaries and rising upwards to the sky. Suddenly, I felt absolutely dreadful. I realised I had visualised the golden light spreading right up to the boundaries of my farm and remaining within the boundaries. Of course, the surrounding land was angry. I had not visualised the golden light spreading *over* the boundaries at will, going wherever it was invited to go.

I tried to explain this to the caller, while desperately trying to put the situation right with the universe. I started picturing the light spreading everywhere like mad, worldwide if it wanted to! I felt devastated at what I had done so unwittingly, and yet I felt totally amazed that these two people had seen the light without knowing anything about what I had experienced.

On the next walk that these two good people took around my boundaries, they were able to confirm that the energy everywhere was now at peace again. I was so, so grateful to them and so happy that the universe only allowed this mistake to continue for a few days before causing me to rectify it! Several other people confirmed the powerful energy and golden light they could see over the farm from a distance. This all acted as huge confirmation to me that all that had been revealed to me was absolutely correct.

Part of the expansion of this story was revealed about two years later, as I lay half awake in bed one morning. I became aware that the animal kingdom can now speed up its 'waking up' process on this farm. I realised several different species of animal that had collected on the farm were wiser souls. They had come to lead their 'kind' into better ways. I could help by talking to the animals whenever I saw a wrongdoing. I had already begun to speak (telepathically) to my ponies and dogs about the way they treated each other. I realised I could now be used, whenever necessary, to speak to *all* the animals I saw and that *I would be heard!* I also saw that this situation could escalate and apply to the plant kingdom too. I resolved to open myself to this awakening phenomenon at a new and deeper level and allow all the teaching possible to come through me.

3

The Second Set of Revelations

Some weeks later, I was doing exactly the same walk I had done on the day I received the first set of revelations, when I felt Dom surround me again. I was overjoyed and this time accepted the situation a lot more readily, feeling our oneness quickly and with joyous ease.

Straight away I fell into a deep trance state and knew in an instant I was experiencing the 'Adam and Eve' moment described in the Bible. Dom showed me that this was the moment the evolution of the planet had reached a very critical 50-50 situation. On the one hand, there was a continual and constant push from the core, prompting us to move forward and find out who we were, and on the other there was a constant learned fear of losing the important balance that had allowed us to survive on earth this far. (I was later to learn that on other planets we had previously incarnated on we had failed to hold this balance.) This situation, combined with the crucial fact that, at this precise moment, precisely 50 per cent of our planet was incarnate (this included rocks, nature, animals, humans, etc.), and 50 per cent was in spirit, had caused a complete planetary 'Split'. This split or shift was the moment that opposites came into the consciousness of every living thing. Opposites had previously been present but we had not been consciously aware of them. These conscious opposites gave each one of us our 'self' awareness. We recognised dark and light, hot and cold, love and fear, little and large, strong and weak, etc. Our senses suddenly became individual to us; our experiences became our own. Our surroundings seemed separate from us. Our bodies became apparent to us and it seemed in that split second that we controlled ourselves. Where we had been selfless beings experiencing an unchallenged oneness with each other, we suddenly seemed to become separate and thereafter filled with our unique 'self'.

In other words . . . *the illusion of the 'I' was born.* And this happened very, very quickly.

Dom allowed me to experience the 'love' side first, which was the side that was still in spirit. The love side remained relatively balanced because it was still in touch with the bigger picture. The souls became self-aware but, at the same time, retained their oneness with each other because they had no form (body) to hide behind.

I was then taken to the 'fear' side and I experienced the moment the incarnated became aware of themselves as individuals for the very first time. I felt shock, terror, bewilderment, guilt, disbelief, anger, fear, in fact a million different emotions coming into being. The moment appeared to strip incarnate beings of their light, spreading what seemed like a real all-encompassing darkness throughout the earth.

Swapping back to the love side again, I could feel the shock running through the spiritual world. Spirits were watching the terrifying state of confusion that was developing on the incarnate side in a blind panic, saying to each other:

'Whatever shall we do? How can we help? We must help. We must keep the balance! They cannot keep the balance for they are in total chaos. It is we who must do something. Panic! Panic . . .'

I was taken back to the incarnate side once more and I experienced the escalating confusion. There were animals and people charging about like maniacs all over the place. Everything 'appeared' very black. I heard screaming from what seemed like every living creature, erupting of volcanoes, earthquakes shaking the ground, animals bellowing, wind howling, trees falling, torrential rain and storms, thunder and lightning. I cannot begin to describe adequately the combined carnage I felt as I dipped into this unprecedented scene from long ago . . . *although, at some level, we all know it, intimately.*

As I re-experienced this moment of the Split, I knew that love was stronger than fear because it was aware of the bigger picture and, for that reason alone, love was always going to be the more powerful of the two emotions.

The situation in which the planet now found itself (50 per cent incarnated and 50 per cent in spirit), continued for some time, the spiritual trying to figure out what it could do about it and the physical side running riot. Our planet was going through an extremely precarious balancing act and the love side had to control that balance as the physical side was unable to. I knew this moment was one of the most important moments in the planet's history and one which we all need to understand, if we are to bring the true light of source back into our living consciousness.

The light that had entered this planet all those millions of years ago had always had the intention of 'knowing' itself, and a dodgy situation of this kind had undoubtedly always been on the cards, in some form or other.

The planet rocked on its delicate pivot point for some hundreds of years. The love side was continually striving to find a way to redress the balance. In some ways, it panicked in its quest and souls initially re-incarnated in quite a random fashion, always with the highest intention but not thinking things through enough to achieve a lasting solution. Some souls on the 'love' side saw their soulmates struggling and shot quickly back into any old incarnated situation, trying to help. This often only served to exacerbate things and left us with more to resolve. (It has only been in the last few centuries that the bulk of the love side has realised the patience game is the better one, and that they can achieve more by not rushing and just assessing each situation calmly.)

At about this point, I became aware that a type of competitiveness had come into being. The only way that rebalancing could begin was from the love side. The fear side was too unaware and out of control, to help. So the love side exerted itself to its highest level and in doing so became a little competitive, in some way seeing 'who' could achieve the impossible first. This desire, this longing from the love side, to achieve, caused a competitive mountain to emerge, and it *had* to be climbed . . .

By this time, I had completed my walk and reached home again. I felt a pressing need to go upstairs and find my Bible. I opened it at the first chapter, Genesis, and read about the 'dark days' described there. I had not read those words for decades and, when I had previously read them, I had not understood them. But on this day, I read on and on in awe, understanding only too well exactly what they were depicting. Very soon I came to the verses on Noah. Here I stopped because I felt myself being strongly drawn away from the biblical pages.

Dropping into a deep trance state once more, I found myself with a group of souls who had gathered on the love side. They had the idea that if they all incarnated together, in a remote spot, at exactly the same time, they would give a united strength to their mission and might in that way achieve bringing light back to the earth. They reasoned that a mass body of incarnated spirits might have more of a chance of recognising each other and therefore be more likely to hold on to their light energy through the difficult transition. At that moment, it dawned on me that the group of souls I was connecting with was Noah and his family. The Noah energy had been the very first part of the love side that had achieved an incarnation on earth without becoming swamped by fear. Noah's family successfully brought the energy that was love/light to our earth in an incarnated state and didn't let the crazy, madly damaged world destroy them. In other words, they were the first saviours of the planet, after the Split. They had done what had seemed almost impossible . . . I sat back in my chair in disbelief!

Noah . . . this man, who to me had only ever been part of quite an insignificant Sunday school story that involved taking pairs of animals into his ark.

Noah!

I started to see this incredibly special moment in greater detail:

Before the Noah energy incarnated, I felt it collecting in spirit to plan the mission. Souls collected who had various different experiences. Some had experienced short incarnations. Some had been close to the planet at the time of the Split, had experienced the fear first hand and then been catapulted back into the ether by the force of it. Some had watched the goings on from afar. But all were souls who were not unduly damaged by having experienced an incarnated state. They all collected to form a plan that carried the best chance of bringing the light back to earth.

It was decided that the souls would reincarnate into a remote region, as far away from any troubles and confusion as possible. A quiet plateau was chosen, near the top of a large mountain range: 50 per cent of the souls decided to remain in spirit to support the mission; 50 per cent were brave enough to reincarnate, each alongside a mate from the opposite sex. Some came as trees, some as other forms of vegetation, some as animals and some as humans. They came in pairs, ready to breed, ready to spread love, each determined not to become swamped by the light.

So the little community supported themselves in this way. As they incarnated, they recognised each other, and while they were going through their own individual experience of an incarnated state, sometimes for the first time, they could tap into support from each other and also from their spiritual counterparts, thus holding the light intact.

At this point, I kept seeing the outline of a hefty wooden ark. I asked what it meant and I was shown that the ark represented the souls on the spirit side who were holding the space safe for the reincarnating Noah energy while they began their mission. The ark was shown as a frame and the incarnating souls were free to go in and out of it, at will. So the Noah energy *had* to face all that incarnation meant but, at the same time, the souls were being supported and held as much as possible from the other side. The two sides *were obliged* to work together to make this experiment work. And the energies had to be at a perfect 50-50 split.

As the enormity of who Noah and his family really were and what they had done slowly sank in, I realised why (in biblical terms) God had sent us a rainbow at that time. It represented his promise never to send any more floods of that nature to earth and a warning that whatever happened in the future, we would have to take responsibility for our actions ourselves. I had always thought it was odd that 'the rainbow promise' should be linked to that event, despite their having been seemingly much bigger events in our history! Now I realised that this *was* one of the biggest event in our history, simply because it took our planet's balance from 50-50 to 49-51, so to speak. It took the world out of immediate danger. I began to see Noah and his family in a very different light than I had ever done before.

Dom took me quickly on to realise that Noah, or the Noah energy, had started the process of rebalancing our planet and we have been busy continuing the process ever since. There have been other great teachers helping us at strategic moments, such as Joseph, Mohammed and Jesus. Each have accelerated our progress in their time and spun us faster along our evolutionary path. I realised our planet is now fast heading towards a much rebalanced state, but this time, as we re-find our balance, we will *know* it.

I'm not sure when, during these revelations (which took seven hours to receive), I became aware that the so called Atlantian and Lemurian eras were the years preceding the Split. I had often had flashbacks to those peaceful earth days, that were filled with love and light. Indeed, I had deep cravings for that existence. But somewhere among what was being shown to me, I became aware that the days of Atlantis (for want of a better word), or the peaceful days, ended at the Split. Some sort of shift *had always been going to happen.* It was part of an ongoing experiment by the universe, to see if the light could retain its balance and yet become aware of itself at an individual level . . . and survive. There was a huge chance it would self-destruct, but, of course, the love side always had the upper hand because it could see the bigger picture. 'Love' was the only chance we had, to help avert the earthly eradication that threatened so dramatically after the Split occurred.

4

How the Revelations Affect us Personally

For those of you who readily accept that we have incarnated over and over again on this planet, first in rock form, then as some kind of vegetation, thirdly as animal and some of us now as human, it could be time to find out who or what you were at the time of the Split. During the Split, we all experienced our very first *individual conscious* emotions and these emotions have dominated all our subsequent lifetimes. The rebalancing of our planet is currently taking the form of realising these things. The more we realise that all the damaged emotions that are stuck in our various pasts have to be released, including, most importantly, our very first individual emotions, on which the others all hinge, the closer we humans come to returning to a balance that will consciously bring back to earth the pure love and light that we once knew. When we fully release our very first emotions, we are able to release everything else that has blocked us ever since and we will be able to serve ourselves and the planet in a truly balanced way.

Souls experienced the Split in every conceivable form. All souls had previously been unconscious light and the shock of the first individual conscious moments impacted on every soul in a different way. I feel very privileged to have shared so many individual experiences of this moment. The people who have come to see me and allowed me to 'see' their experience have allowed me to build an ever-growing understanding of what actually happened, and I'd like to share with you a few examples.

Some souls experienced that first 'darkness' for only a few minutes. When the chaos started, they were only conscious of one or two massively impacting happenings before they transferred back to the spirit side. However, the emotions they experienced usually had a permanent impact of entrapment, fear, terror, shock or guilt. In future reincarnations, souls have re-lived these damaging emotions in various forms, over and over again. At some point during or after birth, something would trigger the 'darkness' again and they would live in confusion, attracting further dark experiences, without knowing why.

Other souls were literally just making their way towards a new incarnation when the Split occurred. Some got catapulted back into the ether and some actually continued the journey and landed very uncomfortably in a physical position they could not comprehend. Some have remained in this stuck state ever since, repeating the experience in some form or other, every time they have reincarnated. These can be extremely damaged people and each subsequent incarnation has often served to deepen the damage.

A lady came to see me who enjoyed making friends with 'walk in' souls but she was not a 'walk in' herself in this life. For those of you who don't know what a 'walk in' is, it is a situation created by someone who can't cope with their life and, at some point, often when they are asleep, they opt out, by leaving their body. Their empty body is immediately taken over by another soul (a walk in) who wants to by-pass the birth process and childhood, and is looking for a quick way into another incarnation.

However, the above-mentioned lady was slightly different. She had always felt she malfunctioned and could not get in touch with who she really was. She asked me if I could see who she had been at the time of the Split and I saw straight away she had been in spirit. She had been one of the souls watching the happenings in disbelief, shock and panic. She could relate to all those emotions very strongly within herself in this life. When it was her turn to attempt bringing 'love' into the incarnate side, she bravely made her way towards earth with an intended mother figure in mind. However, as she approached the earth, she felt an unfamiliar thickness in the atmosphere surrounding her. It appeared to her like a smoky cloud and she lost her way. However, she determinedly continued her journey and unfortunately found herself incarnated in a different body to the one she had intended. This lady then proceeded to tell me how she had continually got lost as a child and how many other things in her life completely reflected her first attempt at incarnating after the Split.

I have come across a few wiser souls who were incarnate as the Split moment approached and were generally held in high esteem. Some of them sensed that a change was coming and tried to hold on to the fast fading light. For them, the darkness that ensued was a gradual process they tried to fight off but eventually could not. They are often to be found living very difficult lives now, feeling that somewhere they have let their fellow beings down. Some have felt they can never have the light back because they lost the battle at the time of the Split and cannot comprehend that the battle is now waiting to be won.

I have tuned in to souls who went completely barmy at the time of the Split. I particularly remember one who's first conscious moment was of animals seemingly attacking him. (In actual fact, they were just rushing towards him in their panic.) As he happened to be holding on to a stick, he lashed out at them, killing some of them as they passed. I remember tuning in to his astonishment at his first experience of death. Until that moment, he had no idea that he could kill. This poor man has reproduced this event in many subsequent lives, always striking out whenever he felt attacked.

There was the soul who formed part of a volcano at this crucial moment in our history. Her experience of the volcano was that she ended up buried in a mountain of molten ash and was unable to breathe. Her only conscious memory was that of being suffocated and buried. Subsequent incarnations have always held her in this same mould and she has re-experienced the moment in differing guises, time and time again.

Some souls feel tremendous *guilt* because of their unique circumstances at the moment of consciousness. Often they incarnate into families that compound this feeling in order to help them remember it. They wholly believe they are responsible for all that is happening around them in some way (even if their common sense tells them otherwise). It is difficult for these people to believe they are not guilty as they tread each new earthly path, and it is only in seeing the bigger picture and the circumstances around which they have built this belief, that they are prepared to allow the root of their guilt to go, eventually realising that, of course, the whole experience of the Split was completely beyond their control. After the root has dissipated, it becomes necessary to break the body's habit of feeling guilty and dissolve any residual energy that is left.

One lady came to see me who was steadily working her way through her past lives but couldn't quite access her emotions at the moment of the Split. Upon being asked to help her, I realised she had been standing under a gigantic natural waterfall and her first conscious emotion was one of 'shock' as she felt the pounding of water upon her head. She then became aware she was cold, being constantly attacked from above (or so it seemed to her) and she became paralysed by the fear of the moment. I saw her being pulled out from under the waterfall by 'a separate energy' and lie gasping on the grass where she experienced a further set of emotions. This was the first time I had felt one soul help another at this very auspicious moment. I was very surprised and asked for confirmation that what I had 'seen' was true. I then realised that an energy from the 'other' side had pulled her out. We both felt it was more than likely to be her twin soul because the two of them still rescue each other from similar situations to this day.

A middle-aged lady came to see me and explained her complete inability to love and how she only felt really at home in nature. As she spoke, it became clear that her heart had shut right down because something was terrifying her. Upon her allowing me to 'see' her moment of the Split, I first saw her as a monkey swinging happily with her family and friends in the trees. The sense of unity, fun, love and happiness was amazing. When the Split came, the monkeys all felt the earth shifting and the tree they were in was swaying madly. First, they clung to the tree in terror but eventually the tree crashed down as the ground opened up at its base. Some monkeys survived, some were killed and some were wounded. The monkey/lady that was with me had been a survivor and when I picked up her emotions at that moment they were of terror, loss, paralysis, confusion and shock. I felt her jumping up and down on the same spot unable to function. When I said this to her, she said: 'That's what I do now. I jump up and down on the same spot! And I must tell you that I turn to trees for solace all the time. And it's very funny but I have always said I could live off bananas. I eat them each and every day!'

This poor lady had not functioned properly since the day the Split had apparently 'robbed' her of everything she held dear. She had been gradually bringing these emotions to the surface through many lifetimes and just as she came to see me they were fully around her. As we were able to reconnect with this crucial event, she was able to let them all go.

Shock impacted on us in many different ways. One very interesting scenario was that of a lady who had been an 'elder' wolf. As (his) first moment of consciousness struck, it was physically too much for his elderly body to cope with and he suffered a heart attack. However, his soul became caught on the ceiling of the cave he had been in. He did not realise he had passed back to spirit as he watched his family go 'bonkers' from his high vantage point. He sensed them grow steadily angrier and start to fight each other in a chaotic manner. As they grew noisier and the howling wind and storms outside the cave grew louder, the wolf soul on the ceiling became consumed with something he didn't seem to be able to escape from. He did not realise he could simply slip out of the cave. He allowed the terror of all that his fellow wolves were experiencing to engulf him. He, in effect, became taken over. He only released when the whole family finally spilled out of the cave and he went with them.

This lady recognised herself in this story, knowing she had incarnated over and over again like an absorbing sponge. She had allowed other energies to cloud her own and therefore couldn't ever function in a clear way. As soon as she understood her wolf existence, she started to unravel her feelings and open herself to releasing all that had happened to her in the most advantageous way.

A wonderful soul came to see me who carried some of the Mary Magdalene energy. When we traced her incredible story back to the Split, we realised she had been in spirit. Her first reaction as she saw the chaos on earth was, 'I must go and help. I must do something. But I don't know which way to go'.

She started to zigzag around in her urgent desire to help. As she zigzagged, she drew closer to the earth and collided accidently with the moon mass. Her energy stayed on the moon for a while, feeling shock, fear, aloneness and helplessness as she watched the growing chaos. Then she became cold as the sun withdrew its heat and everything became dark so she chose to leave the moon and naturally made her way towards earth. She landed in the middle of the ocean as some sort of fish where she continued to zigzag, looking desperately for ways to help. Gradually, she felt cold again and, as she tried to leave (as she had left the moon), she became aware she was in a body. She was unable to leave. A panic gripped her. She could no longer feel her connection to 'source'. Panic was closely followed by fear and anger at a much deeper level than she had felt on the moon. She felt the heavy weight of the body and the aloneness of her state. She felt trapped. This entrapment led her to go slightly demented in that life and she never recovered.

This lady had lived her whole life (and indeed all her lives since the Split) in the same state of panic. It had driven her and those around her into a frenzy as she searched in anger and frustration for her lost light. She felt a tremendous connection to the moon and had felt governed by it. She looked for light/love in every conceivable place instead of remembering it was within her. As she started to reconnect with her story and her inner light, a calm spread over her and the panic receded. An understanding of her whole life (or, rather, lives) fell into place.

A very disturbed lady visited the retreat and I could feel she had awkward mental problems and difficulty in living. She had spent many years going from one therapist to another. As I listened to her, I realised she lived the 'Split' scenario every moment of every day. I was astonished she should be so openly trapped in it. Upon asking the universe for clarification, I realised she had been a type of bee, flying, at the actual moment we all became conscious. She continued flying, wondering why she couldn't seem able to land. Everything suddenly felt very different to her and she flew close to every plant she encountered, taking in its energy, trying to find a place where she felt safe. She grew more and more tired, and fear engulfed her as she appeared to be stuck in no man's land. Where was she? Where was 'home?' Eventually, she became so tired she fell to the ground and rolled a few times before coming to a standstill. At that point, in rather a stunned state, she became aware of herself and her body. She continued the rest of that life in the same disorientated state, neither feeling part of the incarnate world nor part of the spirit world but rather somewhere in between. The fear and disorientation that had engulfed her as a bee had remained, crippling every incarnation she had had since, causing her to experience bizarre situations over and over again. She had also absorbed 'other' energies every lifetime, reliving her bee existence and desperately searching for her 'home'.

This lady had one of the clearest visions of the 'approaching' shift I have ever encountered. She could feel its vast significance and experienced it in a deep and meaningful way in her everyday life. She understood it so well because she lived her 'Split' experience so constantly. Therefore, the two shifts (the Split and the approaching shift) correlated perfectly for her. I knew her complete healing would take quite a while because she had absorbed so many different energies, but at least she now understood it all and would be able to gradually free herself. I commented to her that it was almost as if she had lived with a foot in both worlds, with a Split down her centre, and she agreed.

A man came to see me who had been in the thick of the Hillsborough disaster. As he related the emotions he had experienced, I knew he was recounting the exact emotions he had experienced at the time of the Split. I asked him if he would like to understand why he had attracted his Hillsborough experience. He then allowed me to see his first moment of consciousness and I felt him sliding down the side of what seemed like a hole that was forming in a cliff. There was rubble and rocks, plants and small insects sliding down with him. I felt his terror of being 'out of control'. He had landed at the bottom of the hole and, as all the other rocks and debris landed on top of him, he was soon buried. He had felt helpless and kept asking himself, 'What has happened? How did this happen?'

The man then went on to tell me he had lived his entire life trying to stay in control of every situation. He was terrified of losing control. It had ruined a relationship and his jobs, and was impacting on many other things in his life. As he understood why he felt like this, he was able to release his fear and begin to understand exactly who he was and why.

More often than not, souls who were with each other at the time of the Split, have come together in this particular lifetime in order to heal their initial experience. Sometimes a light soul has particularly chosen to spend time with a very dark soul in order to grow, but more especially to bring light and dark together into a new incarnate situation, in which they are forced to heal.

A lady came to see me who I could have likened to a sinking ship. It became obvious to me very quickly that she was a very light energy who had reincarnated at this time, not because she *had* to but because she chose to. She had selflessly chosen to marry a man who had killed her in a previous life, wanting to help him heal. More than that, at the time of the Split, he had just been approaching the earth surface when the tectonic plates shifted and he had spiralled out of the earth very suddenly, causing his energy to form a powerful whirlwind. The whirlwind had uprooted a tree as it spiralled upwards, and caused it to fly through the air. It then landed heavily back on the earth, where it died shortly afterwards. This lady had been the tree.

The initial emotions that each carried were completely opposite to one another. The whirlwind felt a power and control and the tree felt powerless and out of control. The two were mirroring this same scenario in this life. As soon as I explained to the lady that she had come to recognise this moment and to heal it, she started to beam her light outwards and heal all the emotions she had come to heal.

Quite often, I come across souls who were animals caught up in some sort of huge frenzy. Some were unhappily being killed and some were the actual killers. Every time the soul and I 'see' the event that occurred, it is always very dramatic. Often, the frenzy remains within the psyche and is difficult to release because so much of the energy is not their own.

Many of the souls (but not all) I have come across so far, who have reached the point of being able to comprehend the 'Split', are gentle souls. Those who had a violent experience at the moment of the Split often shy away from these understandings, but they should not. No one could help where they were at this moment; its timing was completely random as far as each individual was concerned. Therefore, no one should be held responsible for actions that were unavoidable. If we had known what was happening and could have reasoned our way through the event, we would probably all have behaved quite differently. But, of course, we had no idea what was going on and could only live with the ensuing consequences.

No living thing should ever be held unforgivably accountable for anything they have done, for it was all done in ignorance and it is only ignorance that still holds them captive. Karma, of course, has to be completed and it may be that some souls can only complete their karma once they have understood where they were at the time of the Split. There is no set order as to how we all progress.

We are all a part of the whole process and are therefore equally responsible for helping each other become free from our own particular wounds. Our own circumstances were such because the planet reached a 50-50 balance and we happened to *be* 'wherever we happened to *be*'. The first moment of consciousness was terrifying for us all and the impact felt then and now should be released with time, patience and unconditional love.

Many, many souls are now working through the various lives that they have had which have caused devastation and severe damage to their beings. When they finally come to the place where they can access their first experience of individual emotion, they understand why everything has happened to them and, in that knowing, they can set themselves free.

The importance of the Moment of Consciousness is further understood by knowing that many collections of souls today that were 'one soul' at the time of the Split and experienced their first emotions as one, are reuniting again now, after many, sometimes thousands, of years of separation and different experiences. They are incarnating together at the present time in close proximity, for example as family or friends, even workmates, some working from the non-physical side and some from the physical. This is happening to enable them to recognise each other again and heal; the healing process allowing them all the opportunity to reach the root of their first emotions and gain further understanding of our evolution.

The souls that are coming together are all helping each other in this deep healing process. Sometimes these souls show up as people we feel a discomfort with. But we need to encompass 'all' in our quest for understanding, because until 'all' who made up each unique soul at the time of the Split are reunited and growing, we cannot heal ourselves fully. Our collective soul can only be as light as the least light soul in our group.

Some souls in our current lives are beings that caused us terrible damage at the time of the Split or are souls that we damaged. We have come together at this time to heal all the damage, to understand it and to forgive it in all aspects. Each time this happens, more and more light returns to the earth.

Taking these enormous thoughts one step further, our whole planet is only as evolved as the least evolved soul that exists. The more evolved souls must eventually assist the least evolved souls to pass through the 'eye of the needle' for, of course, we are all 'one' at source!

If you are able to remember your own 'Split' experience by tuning into past lifetimes, or if someone else can aid you, then some of these simple basic guidelines may be of use:

1. Ask for all the damaged emotions that you hold from this moment, and all subsequent lifetimes, to be healed as soon as possible.

2. Forgive those who have hurt you and ask for forgiveness for anyone that you may have hurt throughout all your lifetimes. Forgive yourself too.

3. Ask for all those who were around you at the time to be healed and helped in the highest possible way. Allow the universe to use you as you grow in your understanding, in any way that will aid this process.

4. Thank all those souls who have collected around you in this lifetime, to help you heal your Split experience.

5. Remember that having *seen* your first emotions, you need now *only* heal from there. Every emotion that now troubles you can be sourced back to that time. Ask for all that can be healed to be healed and leave the door open for more healings whenever they come.

6. Ask to be rebalanced at every level.

7. Ask for help to become selfless again, as you were before the Split occurred.

Only ask these questions once. If you hold on to a question, the universe cannot respond. By asking and *letting go* . . . you will get your answers.

5

My Own Experience of the Split

'Fear is the unknown.'

I have been slowly putting together my own experience of the 'Split'. Different pieces of it have been shown to me at different times and I still don't know if there is more to come. However, it currently runs something like this:

At the exact moment of the Split, I was in my mother's womb. She was several months' pregnant. I believe I was a lion cub. My first memory was a stifled feeling of trying to breathe through my nose and finding I could not. I remember becoming aware I was confined tightly in a small, soft, dark, fleshy space and knowing the environment in which I was held was somehow altering. I became aware it was dark and I was trapped. I recall the unexpected shift from the peace, love, security and calm I had been experiencing as quite the norm, to the onset of confusion and fear. I felt it through my mother's womb while, at the same time, I still felt very protected and safe. I know I 'logged' this change and I strained every nerve and sinew to try and understand what had happened. This caused an extreme tension to grow within me. Somehow I recognised it was hopeless to try and understand why everything was changing. I simply remember knowing I could do nothing about it at that moment but I was still safe. I simply had to experience the change from where I was. I was left in a state of confusion and worry but I totally trusted all would be well.

Two months or so later, I was born. By this time, creatures had begun to recognise like for like. In other words, the same breeds were beginning to collect and either co-habit or fight each other. I remember emerging into this changing world, feeling very lost and vulnerable without my mother's immediate protection and thinking to myself, 'This wasn't what I was expecting. Where am I? Where *is* the world I was expecting? What has happened?'

Nothing felt right. My mother felt familiar but she was tense and ill at ease. I could hear lots of different noises and feel 'worry' all around me. My surroundings appeared dark and I could feel an all-consuming and overwhelming fear. I smelt death but I didn't know what it was. Drums were beating in the distance with an ominous drone. Everything around me seemed amiss and I didn't know why. In my heart I was searching . . . . searching. Where was *my* world?

A couple of months after my birth, I remember dozing in a type of natural leafy hammock amongst some branches. I opened my eyes to see a *massive* white lion approaching me. He had a smaller female lion with him, though she was hanging back slightly. He raised himself up to his full height at the sight of my 'golden energy' and from this position, close to my face, I heard him emit the most enormous roar. The emotion I felt emanating from the lion was an all-encompassing, ferocious anger. I was somehow aware of my mother running from the scene. I was also aware of the female lion watching from her stance behind the massive lion. I started letting out a terrified high-pitched roar and the lion tore me to pieces . . . And that was it! I guess I was eaten! I certainly passed swiftly back to the other side.

As I drifted out of my cub body in a state of total shock I remember traversing slowly, from side to side, across the eventful scene, aware of a huge mass of lion energy just beneath me, some of which was white and some golden. The primary emotion I felt was terror at its most extreme. There was an enormous battle was going on between the white lions and the golden lions. I didn't know it at the time but the white lions had attacked the golden lions whilst the golden males were away. The white lions were furious that the golden lions (wise ones) still retained some memory/light energy from before the time of the split and in their fear of being 'seen' they felt compelled to eradicate the seemingly threatening golden energy. Therefore an unequal battle was being fought. Some of the golden females and young cubs fought valiantly, some watched helplessly nearby and some simply fled the scene. The white lions had carefully planned the attack and were always going to win. They successfully killed off the female and younger golden lions and later picked off most of the golden males individually. This battle was one of several that took place world wide and marked the end of the existence of any remaining embodied enlightened energy.

From my elevated position I looked for my carcass and in the mangled mess of remains I saw a piece of golden coat that I knew was part of my former body. I stared at the furious fight going on around it and started to pick out the energies of many members of my family in this life. Some were white lions and some were golden. I was amazed at how many of my current family I could identify.

I will relate the following important points:

When the white lion that killed me first saw me, he was immediately filled with uncontrollable anger at the light energy that I retained and this made him attack. He felt a great need to extinguish the light, and this need was driven by fear of his own exposure. So, in his fear, (he thought) he overpowered the light. The white lion, for those of you who have read my first book (*From Chrysalis to Butterfly*, 2008), was Derek. For a long time after this, I re-lived this terrifying scenario on almost a daily basis. People often attacked me because they didn't like what I mirrored back to them. I have now asked for all the fear from this moment to leave me. I wish to be fully healed from this event so I no longer attract attack or react to it, in an imbalanced and fearful way.

When Derek towered over me in a similar way in this life, of course I re-lived the terror of that first conscious incarnation and that is obviously why I almost died. He appeared to tower above me in his anger as he had done so long ago as a lion, although neither he nor I were conscious of this at the time. But I now realise that something in our conversation must have triggered an old memory and he started attacking the 'light' in the same way.

It took me a long time to realise that the mother I saw running away from the lion scene had reappeared as a friend in this life. I didn't fully realise that this part of the events had had such a deep impact on me until I started to look at why she should now be hurting me over and over again. I became aware that as I had watched her running from the scene (from a space outside my body), I had never thought to forgive her. I then re-lived the scene through her eyes and knew I would probably have reacted in the same way she had, if I had been in her shoes. I immediately felt forgiveness and understanding flood through me.

Knowledge of what my mother had subsequently gone through came to me at a later date. She had run around in a terrified way until she teamed up with an aggressive, strong male with whom she found a form of shelter from all that was happening. He became her protector, and even though he was an aggressor she felt safer with him than she had on her own. And as she calmed herself I felt her become conscious of tremendous sorrow and guilt for having run from her kin. She continued to live—dominated by those emotions, for the rest of that life.

Unfortunately, this 'mother' is still running in this life, dominated by those same emotions . . . . I asked that she should be helped to heal from all that had happened in every possibly way, should she one day be brave enough to face herself.

As I further traversed the scene of the fight from my disembodied state I saw several pairs of eyes peering out from behind some bushes. On closer inspection I realised one pair belonged to my daughter/younger sister (who were one and the same energy at this time). They were a young female golden lion who had 'married' a male white lion. As they peered out through the bushes I knew they were full of mixed feelings as to where their loyalty should lie. They felt tremendous guilt that they were not helping their own kin but they were too frightened to go against their mate. Going against their mate seemed to mean certain death.

As I relived this scene from long ago I felt deep anger and shock at my daughter/sister. How could they not help us in our terrible plight? How could they hide and watch us all suffer? I remembered the anger I felt as I drifted further away into the ether and it unfortunately stayed with me. Looking back on the scene as I was now, the pain I relived was almost unbearable. I tried desperately to forgive them but it was so deep I was finding it hard. Then suddenly I put myself in their shoes and realised *I* could have been the one who had been married to a white lion and felt a split allegiance. I then relived the intense fear that was theirs at the time. I knew I would have done what they had done if I had been them. I felt a massive rush of forgiveness throughout my body—and as I did so the pain lifted, and the sadness and anger left me unconditionally.

Now when I think of my sister or my daughter I know that they are forgiven at this deep and most important level and that they will feel this forgiveness in their higher selves and come to a full healing in their own time. The ugly energy that I held from that time is at last released.

I gained immense insight about one of my uncles when I recognised him as a white lion. Upon asking for further understanding I realised his wife and children in this life were all present at the same terrible fight and I went deep into their story to release as much as I could. I found I could understand much of their behaviour patterns in this life and found myself forgiving my uncle on behalf of many members of the family. This was mostly led by my aunt who is currently in spirit and she and I managed to release huge chunks of their history. I was bringing it to consciousness and she would be able to use the energy to help forgive and heal them.

At one point I had the realisation that the female lion who had stood behind Derek was his wife in this life. She had watched the whole scene in that life and had similarly watched the repeated version in this life. She is still watching the scene, and I have often wondered why. I had asked her several times to help Derek understand his part in the story, to no avail. However, after recently realising where she had been at the time of my lion cub death, I understood why she was not attempting to help Derek through his part of the healing process in this life. There was a part of her that held some guilt, and therefore she was giving a misplaced sense of loyalty to Derek, even though she had actually done nothing but watch.

One day Dom appeared and asked if I would forgive him for not being around to protect me as a cub and similarly forgive him now for not being here for me in this life. He had wished to be here with me, he had intended to be here. My thoughts slipped back to the day Derek attacked me. Dom had protected me initially when Derek first came and accosted me. He had then left me to finish my walk alone, thinking I was safe, thus leaving the opportunity for Derek to attack me again. I realised history had repeated itself. Dom, the father lion, had thought I was safe when he left me in my hammock! I then understood even more clearly why Dom now chooses always to be here for me in spirit. He feels it is the best way for him to put things right. As I had already forgiven Dom for everything, this little interlude served only to give me more clarity for which I was very grateful.

The emotions that I listed when I was in the womb are very much key emotions that I have lived with throughout this lifetime . . . I have lived this and probably all my other lives feeling trapped inside my skin. For some considerable time, I felt my skins were gradually releasing but of course did not realise I was actually releasing the moment of the Split. The most important aspect of this is that I have been blaming my own skin for the trapped feeling and I now know it was my mother's womb that was 'apparently' trapping me and *my* skin was never a trap. Therefore, I can live in my own skin happily now.

My family have always described me as being a very tense person. One morning, I woke up knowing the tension came from the two months of waiting in the womb, not knowing what was going on. I was born in that life feeling that extreme tension and I have unfortunately felt it ever since. When I asked for that tension to be released, it seemed as though an enormous spring released from my body and suddenly I found myself telling my body it did not need to be tense any more. I knew I did not need all the minor aches and pains in my body and I asked them to go. (I have been a different person ever since.)

I also realise why I felt so lost and vulnerable when my mother died in this life. I have always felt the need to be cradled, protected and loved by a mother figure because that was how I felt in my mother's womb at the first moment of the Split. But now I can stand alone, understanding at the deepest level where those strong emotions/needs came from.

I recognise that throughout all my lives I have been desperate to bring the true light back to earth. I have been confused by the world around me. I have felt the fear in the same way as I did back then and I have known it shouldn't be that way. I have yearned for the world I remembered, the world before the Split.

I have always been wary of small tight spaces, but not allowed myself to be overcome by them. Therefore, I can ride in lifts but I have to detach myself from the perceived danger in order to do it. I can go into small spaces like attics, but with difficulty. I am unable to go under water with any ease at all. I hate the feeling of water filling my nose. I used to think it was because I had drowned in a past life but I now know for sure that it is a similar feeling to the one which I had at the initial moment of consciousness in the womb (the feeling of being unable to breathe).

I have always been puzzled by the world and expected it to be a better and nicer place than it is. I naively trust everyone and go around with an innocence that is quite ridiculous for my age. I know now that I live constantly as I did the moment after I was born in that first conscious life. I feel that energy, I live that energy, I am that energy . . . and I am always searching through the confusion of life for answers.

Drums tend to have a disruptive effect on me and I feel the sound like an invasion, a wrecking of my peace, and an uneasy, uncomfortable, eerie sound. And when something 'black' comes at me . . . I tend to 'die' inwardly . . . just as I did, so long ago.

The understanding of these events has helped me to understand myself, my purpose and my journey through my lifetimes, so much better. I continue to get stronger and clearer with each moment.

I am an avid seeker of the truth . . .

When I was in the womb, I did not know what had happened and had to wait until I was born to partake in the unfolding drama. After my birth, nothing was as I had imagined and, therefore, from that moment on, I began searching for the 'light' that I had been expecting.

In the life I lived when Jesus was alive, I can remember being a merchant who travelled from country to country, always restless and on the move. When I glimpsed Jesus for the first time and recognised the 'golden light' that emanated from him, it was as if a dream I had always had was suddenly becoming a possible reality. I followed him all the way up the Via de la Rosa, fascinated by what I was sensing, and stayed close to him as he died on the cross. From his death onwards, I searched for truth in every nook and cranny. Who was this man? Who knew this man? Who could tell me about this man? Why had he died? What had he done? And I relentlessly pursued his disciples, his family, his followers, his tracks, giving my life to the search, trying to make peace with that something that was missing in my heart and knowing he somehow held the key. I *knew* without a shadow of a doubt that Jesus was the connection to something I had lost.

In all of my subsequent lives, I have always given my life to the 'cause'. That was why my first mission in this life, as soon as I was old enough, was to search for my own truth, before I could begin to serve in any other way. It explains why my passion for the truth is still the uppermost thing in my mind. I will not rest until I have the whole truth within my incarnated being, and from that state I will help to light the world.

My personal part of the current 'great plan' partly came about as a result of where I happened to be at the time of the Split. I have recently discovered that I also formed part of the 'light' energy that finally achieved an incarnation with Noah. Each and every one of us will be dominated by our first emotions until we fully understand them, move through them, releasing every aspect as we go. This is part of the great ascension process that is bringing more and more conscious light back to our planet.

In one of my first incarnations after the Split, I can remember living in a dark, damp cave. The cave was a very basic home with carcasses strewn around the floor and skeletons hanging on the walls. Derek was my husband/ partner and I could sense that we had a few children. He was the breadwinner and he spent a lot of his time out hunting. I was left alone all day, looking after the children. I recall we did not wear much in the way of clothing, mainly animal skins around our groins.

One day he came back to our cave and I can remember crying for some reason. He raised the weapon he was holding, his whole body was full of an unreasonable anger, and he killed me. I now understand why I attracted this attack.

The importance attached to remembering this life is because of what happened afterwards. When we had both once more returned to the non-physical side, we reviewed what had happened between us. We both understood that in order to help heal the world and ourselves, we would have to heal all the emotions we had both incurred, throughout both those lifetimes. This would have to be done over a number of incarnations, but we both made a firm pact that this is what we would do. We knew it would always take the form of 'light meeting dark' and that each time we met, things would be very, very hard, but when our mission was complete, in some way *our* bit of light would be returned to the planet.

When Derek towered over me on that fateful day during this life (Delves, 2008) and I reacted the way I did, we were in fact completing one of the last pieces of our jigsaw. We were bringing the first incident of the white lion back to the fore and we were doing it because I was in an evolved enough state to comprehend the situation and would therefore be able to heal the past forever.

I have indeed understood our story though, as yet, I have not been able to communicate this to Derek.

Whether I ever do or not is irrelevant to me for only the universe knows the plan for Derek's life. However, my full understanding of the story brings full release of our part of the dark energy that was created at the time of the Split. Light has finally conquered darkness, as it always will, and now there is nothing but love remaining.

The importance of sharing this information is because so many other people at this moment are meeting similar counterparts. Light energies are choosing to incarnate and dwell among relevant dark energies in order to bring healing to bear from the time of the Split. These brave souls who are trying to bring light to our planet in the most painful of circumstances *intend* not allowing the dark energy to 'win'. Men and women are finally having to stand up to each other at this very deep level—the level of the Split.

The dark *is* thinning and light *is* returning.

And so I return to the statement, 'Fear *is* the unknown'.

When I was sitting in my mother's womb in love, peace, security, and so on, I didn't know it. I only knew it when the Split altered all our perspective and gave us consciousness. Then, and only then, could I look back and see what I had been. So I have to bless the *hell* that became our earth at that time and, furthermore, I bless the fact that we are bringing heaven (light) ever closer again, this time knowing what we are doing.

6

Another Soul Shares her Experience of the Split

I have already told you that where we were at the time of the Split is extremely important. Add to that: who we were, why we were, what we were and the knowledge of whether we were incarnate or in spirit. But more important than anything else, as we come to understand the moment of the Split, is to *experience* the moment for ourselves, once more. It is only in the personal re-experiencing of our own moment that we come to understand just what that moment did to us, and at the same time it will help us understand the moment that light entered the planet at source.

For me, living this moment and re-experiencing it brought an *understanding* of the planet and its purpose, such that I had never known before. It also brought a personal sense of my own journey. I saw the connection between the moment when the light became trapped at source and the moment when I became consciously 'trapped' in the womb. And I understood the illusion of it all in even greater depth. As I emerged from the womb, the 'light' I met gave me a feeling of recognition of what I thought had been taken from me when I was in the womb. I 'saw' the light for the first time and I mistakenly started to look outward for the light. And then I understood! I recognised that it was an illusion. I knew 'I' was the light, I always had been, and that the planet we could see through our eyes, that we could smell, touch, hear, etc., was an illusionary playground.

When people come to see me, I always know when they are ready to explore who or what they were at the time of the Split. As we begin by asking the universe for clarification of their story, the person involved quite often sinks into a state where they can re-live the experience for themselves. More often than not, I sink with them and this enables the person to have the confidence to go 'all the way'.

Every time I have been privileged to share this experience with someone, the moment has been extraordinary. They suddenly come to understand so much about themselves and see the pattern in their lifetimes and why things have happened. One such person has very kindly agreed to share her experience with us here in her own words.

Felicity's Story

I had known for some time that I needed to start tackling the reason why I could not feel love. I had never been in touch with love and, despite tackling many other areas of imbalance in my life, I had never faced this aspect. I started asking the universe for help. And help came . . .

I called at the farm to collect some boots I had left behind on a previous visit. I was talking to Anna about something that had happened recently with a friend of mine and somehow our conversation got deeper and deeper. She had been offering for several months to have a session with me as she could detect that all was not well. In the past, these sessions have often been uncomfortable and I have never felt totally at ease with them. I felt I was nearly always the 'bad guy' and having to accept home truths I would rather not acknowledge. I had been putting off the current problem, sensing it was very deep and, quite frankly, I was scared. My life seemed quite comfortable and settled, thank you very much, and the last thing I wanted was another major soul-searching upset.

Perhaps because we hadn't arranged anything—but, in retrospect, more likely because the universe had answered my prayers and we had been thrown together at exactly the right moment—I didn't brush Anna off. She started by saying that my aura was grey and asked if I would like help in working out what the problem was. I knew I wasn't at ease with myself, so I said, 'Yes'.

She sunk into a trance state and said almost straight away that she could see me on a hillside. I was a shepherd with a crook in my hand and my sheep were scattered all over the hills surrounding me. She could not sense any other human around but she could feel the tremendous empathy and telepathic communication I had with my sheep.

As Anna described this scene, I felt an immense association with it. It felt very familiar. I have always loved walking alone among the sheep in the mountains of Wales. I have often said I would like to live in the Welsh mountains with a dog and with a mountain to climb right outside my front door. I also adore my sister's two dogs and have a special relationship with them. I can't bear to see any animal in pain but I would love to have an animal of my own one day. I have only recently realised that I have never had sole responsibility for any animal and how scared I am of the emotional attachment that owning an animal would entail.

As Anna spoke, I felt such a warm comfortable feeling of recognition. It was as if she was describing something I remembered doing in this life. I really did feel as if she was telling me about my life and the really amazing thing was that I could associate with the feeling of loving my sheep and being at one with them. It was a feeling I could never remember having experienced before. It was wonderful!

Then Anna said she could sense something momentous happening. I had a vision of a wolf coming and taking one of my sheep. Anna continued without knowing about my vision. She said: 'I can feel something so big and painful about to happen that it's almost unbearable. It's something along the lines of a loss of trust between you and your sheep.'

As she was speaking, I felt it as blame. Something had happened to one or more of my sheep and I felt them all looking at me with accusing eyes. I had failed to protect them! She then said, in a rather awed voice, that she thought she was seeing the moment of the 'Split' as it had occurred in my life.

I realised Anna was describing my loving and happy life being shockingly disrupted as the Split occurred, robbing me and my sheep of all that we knew, as we became conscious. I was immediately faced with accusing eyes, loss of trust and loss of oneness and love. It felt as if I had subsequently struggled through all the rest of my lives looking for that love and never regaining it.

All this resonated very deeply within me. I felt able to accept that something had happened many lives ago that had appeared to remove love from my life. It was such a relief to realise there was a reason *why* I struggled so much and that it wasn't my fault.

Anna then stood in front of me and said: 'Try and see what else you can remember from that life.'

I immediately saw a very bright light a long way into the distance. It was like a small torch burning very strong and white. I described it to her.

She asked: 'What do you think that light is?'

The phone rang at that moment, giving me a chance to consider her question. My initial thought was that the light was God. I think this was conditioned by books I have read about near-death experiences where people walk towards bright lights. I then thought that maybe the light was 'love'.

When Anna came off the phone, I told her this and she said to me: 'Try and see which way the light is flowing. Is it flowing away from you or towards you?'

I detected a flow and, in rather a forlorn voice, said: 'It's going away from me.' A moment later, I said: 'Oh! That's the right way!' The love was actually flowing outwards from me to the 'great outside'!

I cannot tell you what a dramatic moment that was. It was the very first time in this lifetime that I felt I had the ability to love! I actually felt love inside me and it was able to flow out to others. Anna told me it had been there all the time but it had got blocked in. My body was racked with sobs of joy and amazement. The dog on my lap must have wondered what was going on as I hugged and kissed him on the top of his head. I can remember saying to Anna that it was as if a block of ice somewhere inside me (I think in my heart area) was cracking.

Shortly after this, I drove home and asked the universe to protect me as I had nearly driven into another car at the bottom of Anna's driveway! I drove along feeling love for *everything*. I loved the fields, the trees, the sky . . . I loved everything I looked at. I gave thanks to God, of course, and felt such an abundance of love in my heart that it was almost overwhelming. I mused that if a policeman stopped me, I would probably just smile at him and possibly even thank him if he gave me a ticket!

Later that day, and the next day, anyone I met got a hug. When I was asked how I was, I would say: 'Absolutely brilliant, on top of the world, thank you.' I smiled at everyone and sent love to everyone I thought of.

It was a couple of days later that I got the first attack of diarrhoea. I had eaten soup at lunchtime and wondered if it had been a bit rich. It seemed unlikely as four of us had eaten the soup and only I was affected. But something caused me to dash to the loo three times in quick succession! For the next week or so, I continued to have loose bowels. I was not ill in any way and I could only assume that it was a part of my emotional release.

Anna said that it is up to me whether the feeling of abundant love remains and for how long, but that nothing can take away the healing from the knowledge I had been given. So while the intense feeling of love has somewhat faded, I am conscious that I have retained the love in my heart and my approach to life and people has changed.

One year after my experience with Anna, it has struck me that going back to remember the moment of the Split with her is not the end of the story. On a number of occasions, that moment has come back to me, sometimes in a very dramatic way.

For more years than I can remember, I have had problems with my neck and shoulder. Earlier this year, I got to the stage where I was feeling that life was hardly worth living with the constant pain and a friend recommended I should visit her cranial osteopath. Laura was fully booked, so I saw her son Nigel. The first few treatments were very gentle, and while my body had quite a strong reaction in the few days after the treatments, my neck and shoulder did not improve. I became aware, however, that there was a strong link between the painful area, my sacrum, and the opposite knee and leg. Nigel worked on all these areas in turn.

At one point, Nigel was trying to work intensively with my sacral area and was getting nowhere. He said it felt very heavy and locked solid. In most of my sessions, I had been trying to make myself relax and be open to healing, often asking the Universe to enable me to benefit from whatever my therapist was doing. Suddenly Nigel said, 'Try imagining a beam of light coming into your sacrum'. So I imagined a strong beam of light coming down vertically right into my lower tummy and through into my coccyx. Almost immediately, Nigel said, 'Ah, that's better'.

It was the most extraordinary moment. It was the first time in my life I had proof that something I had invoked and was visualising really did have a physical effect. There was no question of it being wishful thinking or imagination; it was actually felt by someone else.

As we developed a rapport and closeness, I found I was able to tell Nigel about my experience of the Split with Anna. He listened and seemed to take it all in. Several weeks later, he told me he had tried the light technique with a couple of other clients. The results had not been as dramatic as with me, but there had definitely been a small shift.

In due course, I felt I needed to tell him how my interpretation of what had happened during the Split had changed a bit. I had been doing a lot of thinking about what had happened with Anna. When she said I had experienced something so awful it was almost unbearable, I had had a vision of a wolf coming and taking one of my sheep, and I had felt the other sheep blamed me for not protecting it. Well, my new thinking was more along the lines that it might have been a lamb that was taken, and it was the love that the mother had for her lamb, and the love that the other sheep had for it, that had been taken away. I was directly responsible for destroying the loving relationships within the group which is why I had such issues with love now.

I can recall starting to say, 'Remember what I told you about the time of the Split when I was with my sheep . . . 'I then remember trying to recall exactly what my new thoughts were, but before I could put them into words, Nigel, who had one hand under my bum, suddenly put his other hand strongly and firmly on my lower tummy, exactly over the place where the scar from a former operation itches the most. At the same moment, I felt something bubble up from deep inside me and erupt like a volcano. It came out as deep racking sobs which I was completely unable to control. It was absolutely involuntary and overwhelming and went on for quite a while. My whole body was consumed by it, and throughout the whole process Nigel kept his hand where he had put it. In retrospect, it is extraordinary that he wasn't so shocked by my reaction that he felt he had to jump back and remove his hand. As the sobs subsided, they were replaced by the long shudders one gets after prolonged and intense crying. I felt dizzy even though I was lying down. This felt most odd. Normally, if you feel dizzy you lie down and it goes away. Nigel removed his top hand but kept his other hand under my backside. He said: 'Sorry, but I felt I just had to do that.'

Nigel kept his right hand in position for a while until he said he wasn't sensing any more change. I could have told him there would be no more today. My body (and mind) was in total shock and I went into a cold and very shivery phase. He gave me as much time as I needed to recover, after which I slowly sat up and then rather shakily stood up. The whole session had taken one and a half hours.

Having made another appointment for two weeks' time, I started to drive home. As I got to the junction that would either take me home or to Anna's, I suddenly felt an overwhelming need to go to the farm. I had not told Anna any of my experiences at the osteopath's, but felt I could no longer keep it from her. She would be so fascinated by it, and she was the only person who would understand what I was saying. It was more than that though—it was a need to be in the calm and gentle ambience of her farm. So I phoned and checked that it would be all right to call in, and arrived 20 minutes later. Anna listened to my tale with interest, and remarked at the end: 'You are teaching them (the osteopaths) something, aren't you'?

I agreed. Although they are already very special people with unusual abilities, I do feel we are beginning to work together, and that by opening up what is going on in my head and emotions, and trying to link it to my body, we are developing a new approach that has the potential to be amazingly powerful.

At the next appointment, we started as normal with feedback from me on what I had been experiencing, and then Nigel's hands under my neck. He sat for a while just sensing the situation, and said: 'Well, this feels quite different.'

He moved to my side and put his arm under my backside. I felt a frisson of fear as I remembered what had happened last time, but then I relaxed. I allowed myself to think about the Split, which is what I had been trying to do when the eruption happened. To my astonishment, when I looked at my sheep, they were exuding happiness and love, and looked as if they were trying to wag their tails! It was such a strong message that either they had forgiven me and the love between us was restored, or perhaps, more likely, it had always been there and my perceived destruction of it was all in my head. I was conscious that I was lying there with the biggest smile on my face as I told Nigel what I was feeling. He was wonderful—I must have sounded completely crazy, but he just said: 'That sounds very significant.'

The message I am trying to get across to you is just how much that moment of the Split keeps coming back into my life. Having 'sorted out' any issue with 'my sheep', the area that is troubling me more and more now is 'the wolf'. A friend of mine has a large, male border collie which has always intimidated me a bit. One day, the dog turned on me and bit me on the hand. I have been quite scared of him ever since, and he appears more and more like a wolf to me. Recently, I watched an episode of *The Frozen Planet* (BBC, 2011a), which featured wolves, and I felt most uncomfortable as I watched them.

Not long afterwards, during a joint treatment with Nigel and his mother, I could hear noises that sounded as if they were in the room, and I had a sudden feeling that 'the wolf' was there. I felt immediate fear. Without being aware of what I was feeling, Laura moved her hands to touch each of my shoulders very lightly. I immediately felt protected and the fear left, and at the same time I heard a dog bark outside the window and I realised there had been no wolf. However, I feel very strongly that the wolf and I still have unfinished business to resolve.

The pain in my neck and shoulder now feels more acute than chronic. It is as if it has come to the surface and now just needs a big push to remove it. I am secure in the love that I have recovered from before the Split but I feel as if I am still in the grip of the trauma of that moment and I have not yet tackled all the fear. I will continue to ask to learn from the moment of the Split and to find balance and acceptance of who I am.

At some point, we will all reach an understanding of the moment of the Split, to a greater or lesser degree. We may describe it in other words, but that doesn't matter. What does matter is that we move safely through the moment and let it take us both backwards and forwards simultaneously, on our life path. The above story highlights how important it is to heal from *all* the emotions that damaged us at the time of the Split and to keep healing them at a deeper and deeper level until we are completely free.

7

The Third Set of Revelations

It has been obvious that the 'people' support around me has been slowly disappearing over the last few years. The last support removal came in early June 2011, when my two trusty friends left the lodge at the bottom of my drive rather suddenly. In return for living there, they had helped me out on the farm, and there was no prospect of anyone coming to replace them in the near future. It took six weeks before a new couple arrived and, by then, I had gone through the busiest time of the farming year.

Diving head first into the problem in my usual way, I asked the universe to teach me all I could possibly learn from this situation. Immediately, I became aware of the deeply entrenched emotional terror within me that hadn't shown itself since two days after my mother died. I traced this terror to its source and found myself at the moment when the light energy at the core of this planet was swirling uncomfortably about, feeling the illusionary trap that light merging with matter produced. At this point, we all had communal emotions. It felt as if the integration of light and matter had given us a situation that was not survivable. We seemed to have lost our freedom.

As the trap deepened in its intensity, the mass of emotion it created swirled about, similar to a Catherine wheel, gradually spinning faster and faster. The outer edge of the light suffered the main brunt of this experience because it was unavoidably weaker than the energy at the centre. As the push to release from this terrible trap became unsustainable, eventually some of the pieces at the edge could hold on no longer. It was as if the central core of the 'agony' being experienced pushed itself beyond its limits and let parts of itself go. These parts were then spun off into the mass that was earth. I was shown that this was the first time that any part of the light energy on this planet had held a dual emotion. On the one hand, the pieces were *forced* to let go because of the speed at which they were spinning and, on the other, they *chose* to let go, feeling they could hold on no longer. However, it must be understood that this choice was actually made by the 'suffering mass' as a whole and had been created by the terror of the moment.

We, mass consciousness, had burst our boundaries.

I knew I had been an edge piece of the light that had been one of the first to let go and had spun off into the mass. Initially, I couldn't feel much as I spun further and further away from the core but as my spinning slowed I became more aware. I remember looking back at the light at the core and thinking:

'Whew! I'm away from the trap! Wow! There is a huge distance between where I was and where I am now. I am tiny . . . where I have come from is huge, and the thick blackness around me is even bigger.'

These were among a huge range of thoughts that I had at the time.

I deliberated. I did not wish to return to where I had come from because I couldn't face the 'trap' again, but if I didn't go back I had to remain alone. The terror of aloneness I felt at this point was indescribable in words. It equalled the terror we all felt at the moment of the Split.

I chose to stay alone. I chose to continue pushing outwards, away from the bulk of the light and where I had been. I chose to pioneer and journey towards what I hoped would be something better. And so the first type of 'identity' began. I identified myself as light, and yet something separate from the main light. In this I found independence and a certain freedom. After the terror of the trap, this seemed worth holding onto. As I travelled onwards, it seemed as though the black mass was continually threatening me. I felt vulnerable and constantly alone. The possibility of attack seemed to come from all directions. Therefore, a different type of fear was arising within me.

Having assimilated this knowledge, I asked the universe if it would be possible for me to heal the terror, the feeling of aloneness and the illusion of separateness I was experiencing at that time. I quickly realised I would have to go 'into' the emotion and, as I thought about all that this would mean, I really struggled to breathe. I was terrified of going back into that trap. How was I to heal?

And then I realised . . . I must re-enter the 'trap of light' but I must re-enter as *conscious* light and not as part of the fearful swirl that I had been. But I then found I only wanted to enter the light if it was pure. I did not wish to enter a tainted light. I spoke to the pure light: 'Would you consider taking me back? Can I clear my part of the taintedness and become worthy? Can I come back *knowing* it is not a trap, now being aware of the bigger picture?'

I then considered that going back to the pure light would perhaps mean going back to anonymity. I was scared. I asked for clarification and it was given to me: it would mean losing my boundaries, losing my independence and it might mean disappearing altogether. The reality of it was all I had always wanted but actually being faced with it at this deep level was another matter. When I had spun out of the original swirling light, I appeared to have found an identity. Would going back into it mean losing that identity and therefore losing existence?

Then I realised that when we die (physically) we do this anyway. We do it so often that when we pass over we subconsciously know exactly what is coming. All I was going to do was encounter the same transformation but I would be *choosing* to do it, *consciously.*

Eventually, I gave up the fight and momentarily entered the 'light'. I had an immediate sense of the prodigal son parable in the New Testament. I felt I was the prodigal son who had returned. There was a feeling of unsurpassed love all around me, a welcome, a celebration, a joy. A banquet was laid out and it was for me.

A while later, I ran my mind back over all that had happened. I understood that when the 'light energy' (us) first entered the planet, we experienced a type of *mass* consciousness. The moment I spun off from the mass, I experienced the first *independent* consciousness. The moment of the Split gave us our first *individual* consciousness.

I looked for a common denominator through it all . . . Of course! Our hearts! Love! Love runs through it all. Love runs evenly at the same pace in the same way through all these trials and tribulations. Love is the constant. Love is light. Light is love. By re-entering the part of the light that was pure, I was taking consciousness into that level of being.

I momentarily felt myself go back into the fear of the emotional swirl I had become so aware of. I asked how I could heal. I immediately felt my heart space again. There was peace. It was the same peace there had always been. It had been there all the time!

I knew that when we (light) had first entered the planet, the balance between heart and soul had wobbled. We had become fearful. Heart became buried (but not lost) in a heap of matter, and soul became buried in a heap of fear. The two seemed separate. And the two seemed to act separately. It was the start of the illusion.

From that level of awareness, I asked for all I needed to become available to me, so I could fully heal.

While out for a walk the next day, I was feeling upset because I so often take the blame unconditionally for things and I had found myself in yet another painful situation. On this particular day, I cried out in anguish:

'Why? Why have I always got to take the flack? Why do I always have to put up with everything being thrown at me when all I send out is unconditional love? I'm so hurt! I'm sick of it. How much longer must this go on for?'

I walked on. I knew that if I wanted to be free of all negative emotion, I needed to understand why I was hurting and go into its centre.

And then I knew. Of course! I had always *chosen* to pioneer. I could have gone back to the core of light instead of spinning off into the ether, at the very beginning of time. Having spun off, I could, at any time, have chosen to rejoin the rest of the light again. But I didn't. And I still don't. I still pioneer. So why am I moaning? I am choosing to do this for the higher good! I *want* to be a pioneer energy. And a pioneer has to take the flack. We are teachers. It's what we do! I know there will come a time when I am fully ready to enter the light on a full-time basis. As I do so, this situation will change.

And, from that moment, I have accepted unconditionally all that is thrown at me. I no longer fear hurt. I rather welcome it, that I may use it to grow.

On another occasion, I felt I should share these latest revelations with a guest at the retreat. In doing so, we shared a moment of realisation that she was energy that had *clung on* to the light as opposed to my energy that had *let go*. Her whole life illustrated this same pattern and she suddenly began to realise why. I looked again at myself and realised I always put up with things until suddenly I 'burst' and then chaos reigns! This is undeniably demonstrated in my first book (Delves, 2011) in my experience with Derek! Now I know why!

We looked at each other and knew that if we chose to merge energies we would start to heal at this very deep level. I would no longer feel the need to burst and she would no longer need to cling on. We could unify in this new understanding and achieve oneness again, both for ourselves and, in time, for the planet. We are gradually achieving this.

Just before I went to Peru, these revelations were expanded yet again. I began to understand the nature of our original existence at the beginning of time—in other words, what is known as the Big Bang.

I was shown 'unconscious existence' or 'thought' likened to a ball. As the ball became more and more desperate to know itself, it thought itself into a state of duality and the original Split took place. The duality/split took the form of matter separating itself from energy. The separation of the two caused matter to burst, breaking itself into millions of pieces and spreading ever outwards, creating the cosmos. Energy ran separately in between, so to speak. The energy was the original 'spiritual' side. Matter became the planets (as we now call them).

Ever since this first Splitting, we (matter and energy) have been trying to reunite, but doing it consciously so we would never again live in the anonymity of the past. We have an intense longing to become whole again. At the moment, we look for wholeness in a partner, not realising we are already all that we need. However, as we consciously reintegrate spirit (energy) and body (matter), we slowly start to remember that divine wholeness. Unfortunately, at every birth we tend to forget the understanding of duality again and believe we are only matter once more. This has also happened nearly every time the 'light energy' has entered or birthed into a planet, with varying results.

When light energy entered the mass we now call sun, millions of years ago, it failed to acknowledge its 'matter' side. Because of this imbalance, it grew only as light. What we see now is the result of that experiment. It shines daily in our lives and reminds us not to do it again. There are many such suns in the cosmos, currently burning themselves out, slowly acting out their mistake.

Contrastingly, when light entered what we now perceive to be a 'dead' planet it failed to bring enough energy through and matter dominated its existence. Light eventually lost out completely and left us with a different type of legacy.

When light energy first entered this planet, it knew not to become over excited and do what it had done on the sun. It also knew not to become overly negative and lose out to the mass. There was a learned and inherent knowledge within us, that in order to survive we had to hold a specific balance between matter and energy. This knowledge in its turn caused the swirl of fearful and panic-stricken emotions that Dom first allowed me to re-experience during my first set of revelations. The swirl was so horrific that none of us has ever wanted to re-enter it again.

But in order to understand ourselves fully, we do need to overcome the fear and re-enter the swirl. We not only need to re enter the swirl but we also need to understand and re-experience the threshold we crossed as we stepped into the planet.

Therefore, we must first heal all that we experienced at the time of the Split when we first became individually conscious. Then we must backtrack to the time when we first entered this planet and heal our emotions from that place. After that, we can slip further back into understanding the realms of the original Split between matter and energy. This allows complete and utter healing, a type of momentary transfiguration, where we re-enter the state of bliss. The significant difference is that we are re-entering our original state *fully conscious.*

When we finally achieve this blissful state, we hold the energy forever. It can never be undone. A sweet fruit once tasted can never be un-tasted.

The more of us who achieve this state, in full understanding, who choose to reunite with the source in this way, thus achieving full enlightenment, the more likely we are to safely complete the tipping of the balance on this planet in the coming months and years.

Winter 2012/2013

During this last Winter I would like you to know that after a huge amount of exploration/healing on my part, I have at last re-become the light energy that I was before I entered this planet. I now live comfortably and consciously in the swirl (life) and shine my pure golden light on everything around me. Of course I feel the pushes and pulls of other struggling souls but I have learnt that those pushes and pulls are *not* mine, and I do not let them affect me any more. I am who *I* am.

I now feel totally balanced. I now feel I have re-attained the status I held when I first agreed to help planet earth all those thousands/millions of years ago. The shock of "duality on a planet" is now almost fully understood and released and I can at last be the help that I always intended to be. As the last remnants of shock, fear, trap, aloneness etc leave me, I can marvel at what we (energy and matter) have been through and remind those who are ready, to reach a place where they too can look back and marvel.

8

Machu Picchu (or Ancient Mountain)

I had been considering a visit to Machu Picchu for around a year and I had made a list of people who intimated that they would like to come with me. However, I had no idea of the revelations that were about to come . . .

I awoke one morning during December 2010 in a trance-like state, with the energy of the Split encompassing me. It was a very strong sensation and I became aware I had been around the Machu Picchu area at the time of the Split. I 'saw' a huge volcanic basin and I knew it had just exploded. There had been a large community living there and the eruption caused the community to become engulfed in rocks and lava. All I could see was the outer crest of the basin and a wonderful dawn coming up from behind that dark crest.

I was told my journey to Machu Picchu could be very special indeed. By making a personal pilgrimage to the area, the universe could use it to bring back an enormous part of the 'light' that had been lost at the time. I could take consciousness up the mountain and, because I had been there at the time of the Split, all sorts of growth would come for me as I remembered things and, at the same time, I would be gifting the planet beyond anything I had ever dreamed possible.

I started to think about the people who had shown an interest in coming too. I knew it was no coincidence they wanted to accompany me. I also felt they would have lived somewhere near the Machu Picchu explosion. Our combined energy could serve the planet enormously and they too could benefit personally, as I would.

Ingrid is someone of a similar age to me who I have known for many lifetimes. I instinctively knew she was one of the people I should invite. I had only known her for about three or four years in this life. She came to me for help in the early days of the retreat opening on the farm. At that point, we recognised each other fairly easily from a previous life. She wanted to come to Peru with me, partly because she knew it was going to be very healing for herself and also because she sensed she was the right person to help me. There is also a great deal of trust between us. Trust isn't something that comes with every relationship, at least not to the depth we have it. That was very important for a trip like this. I knew that Ingrid wouldn't let me down, whatever happened.

It came to me that the timing and arrangements for the expedition would be totally in the hands of the universe. The whole thing was so much bigger than us, that all I had to do was follow my intuition to the letter and it would all go to a perfect divine plan. It was a huge relief!

I knew that if Ingrid and I chose to do this, we would be bringing an enormous chunk of the 'rebalancing' of our planet to fruition at a very important moment in the earth's history. I saw the sun rise over the crest of the volcano and I saw it as part of the dawning of a new era. This new era would start when the planet achieved enough of a rebalance to allow 'light' to be in the majority once more.

And so Ingrid and I started to look at what the different travel companies had to offer. At this stage, there was just the two of us planning to go on the expedition. I wondered how many others were preparing for such missions all over the world . . . silently, busily, dutifully, selflessly. IT WAS AWESOME.

November 2011 (11 months later)

The expedition to Peru was delayed from its original dates by two weeks, by the company we were travelling with. However, I trusted it was taking place in perfect divine timing so we rearranged our lives accordingly and accepted what was on offer. The journey turned out to be a far greater experience than we had hoped for. In fact, it was completely mind-blowing for both of us. Ingrid and I returned home on 5 November and I will now try and relate our experiences as best I can.

As we flew over the Atlantic Ocean to Lima, the capital of Peru, Ingrid and I were so excited and pleased that at last the trip was under way. It was now 22 October and it had seemed such a long time ago that we had made the first plans. Sitting tucked safely into our seats, Ingrid suddenly announced that she knew what the expedition was all about. 'It's about the healing of the Split!' she said. I was both amazed and delighted, for I had shared very little of what I knew with her, so it confirmed to me that she was on the right wavelength and would be a huge asset for whatever was ahead of us. In the event, she turned out to be of far greater assistance than I had dreamed possible. I had no idea just how much information I was about to receive and being able to share it with her as we went along helped me remember it all in far greater detail.

Having spent one night in Lima, we flew over the Andes to Juliaca, which is around 3800 metres above sea level. Around five hours after landing, I began to feel the effects of the high altitude. By this time, we had already investigated an Inca burial site and then driven to Puno on the shores of Lake Titicaca. An hour or so later, I was feeling so bad I even wondered why I had come. Lying flat out on my hotel bed, I sank my consciousness into the fear I felt surrounding me and surmised I had probably hardly ever returned to Peru since the time of the Split. All the fear of facing my old haunts was arising within me. I asked if I could release all the fear and be given all the help I needed to face all that there was to face, at every level. Then I distinctly heard the words: 'Do not be afraid, for I have redeemed you. I have called you by your name. You are mine.'

I lay still for a while longer, feeling the fear leave me, and as soon as I felt a little less dizzy I got up and managed to join the rest of the group I was travelling with, for a light meal. I did not suffer from altitude sickness again.

As I had virtually no recollection of any other Peruvian lives after the Split, other than I knew I had something to do with the Noah expedition, almost everything I remembered, while on the holiday, held the energy from pre-Split days. During the couple of days we spent on or around Lake Titicaca, various interesting Pre-Split memories came back to me:

Animals were never killed in those days. Sometimes they chose to lie down in front of humans and offer themselves as a sacrifice of food. They would then quietly die in front of their chosen humans. Plants offered themselves as food in a similar way. It was all very peaceful, loving and joyful.

There was also no physical sex. Two beings coming together would 'think' themselves into a relationship, thus taking themselves out of the 'alone' state, into a wonderful state of oneness. They would experience a blissful transfiguration as their incarnate bodies completely merged and then fell slowly apart again. At this time, conception could take place if a third party approached the couple and asked to join them. This transfiguration is a mirror image of that which takes place when we finally reunite in a balanced way with the source.

Anyway, back to the trip—I took myself off for a walk at 5.00 a.m. one morning, along the shores of an island situated on Lake Titicaca. I had a longing to experience the sunrise and, as I sat on a hillock, watching the sun come slowly into being, I remembered that the sun was an experiment in itself. Millions of years ago, light had entered the sun planet in the same way that light had more recently entered earth. As it had entered the core of the sun, however, it had been determined to shine its light outwards, in order not to lose itself. In so doing, it 'thought' it had disconnected its root from the source and become *only* light. Hence, the sun was a pure ball of light, burning itself outwards, holding the light energy but without the knowledge of the duality it had gone to seek.

As I watched the sun rise, I knew it was a reminder to all the planets across all the universes that a firm balance had to be maintained if we were to conquer existence. Earth was choosing to 'use' the experiment that was the sun, learning not to make the same mistakes, but at the same time making the best use of the heat and light that it could.

Sitting happily in the sun that morning, I pondered whether I was now free of every attachment I had ever had. As I thought about it, to my surprise, I realised I still had a few simple attachments. I therefore spent some time letting go of anything I could think of. I relinquished my love of the farm completely, knowing in yet a deeper way that I would only remain there if it served the highest good. I thought I had already done this but apparently there was still a small attachment from me! I let go of playing tennis, knowing I would have to stop all together if necessary, despite the fact that I felt I needed my fun time. I let go of the future of the retreat, even though I knew how much it helped people. I understood it wasn't the point! And, finally, basking in the sunlight, I gave up *my choice* in every conceivable form I could . . . I felt completely clear.

On 26 October, we took a coach from Puno to Cusco. I had thought I was in for a long, boring journey and was not particularly looking forward to it. However, as we traversed the high plateau of the Andes, just outside Puno, the landscape felt very familiar and I knew I had lived there before, at some point. I felt a huge affinity with the surrounding mountains as I stared at them through the coach window. I then remembered a vivid dream I had had two years previously.

In the dream, I had been living in a community fairly near the top of a mountain, in a little village made from mud huts with grass roofs. The rains came and flood water streamed from the top of the mountain, down through our village, sweeping away a few of our friends, animals, belongings and huts. We were just picking ourselves up from this frightening incident, when another, much bigger, flood came pouring down from the top of the mountain. This time I found I was on the top floor of what felt like a double-decker bus. My youngest son, Edward, was with me and my mum, Peggy, was driving the bus. There were a few other people with us. The bus was balancing precariously (upright) in the water, when I suddenly saw Darby, our dog, swimming valiantly at the back of the bus, wagging his tail to and fro. I was about to call to mum to stop the bus when I realised that she couldn't. It was already floating and she had no control over it.

We floated down the mountain, concentrating mostly on continuing to keep the bus upright. We felt a big movement and a whoosh of water as someone came up the staircase between the two decks of the bus. I remember wondering: 'Is this my daughter or isn't it? Has she made it or not?'

We anxiously clung on to hand rails in the bus as it floated on. We leant first to one side and then the other, knowing that if we followed our intuition extremely carefully the bus would stay upright and we would all survive the ride. After what seemed like an eternity, the bus came to rest on some dry land in a green valley. Everyone disembarked and stood around feeling shaky. Other buses were landing and their occupants were doing the same thing. The survivors of the flood looked at each other in a type of shocked silence. We all knew we had survived something massive but so many of our family and friends had not. We stood there with nothing but our wet bodies to show that we were alive.

I had always wondered if this dream had been showing me what had already happened or what was about to happen in the future. Now, driving across the high plateau, surrounded by mountain tops, I knew it had already happened in this area. I also knew this was the remote area where the Noah energy had chosen to reincarnate. It was here that the salvation of the world had first begun and here that we had all strived to survive without succumbing to the 'darkness'.

I had a quick vision that there had been many arks built which had saved the Noah energy and they had all started their journey around these mountains. As I gradually remembered back to those bygone days, I remembered how we, myself included, had all been praying desperately for help. We hated the carnage that seemed to reign around us. We felt devastated by the 'dark energy' that enveloped the world we could see. As we prayed earnestly to source for help, the rains came. The first set of rains frightened us all, but, unfortunately, it wasn't enough to halt the carnage. So a second set of rains came. This time it was so severe that everything was washed away, leaving only a few of us to survive in our arks. (This was the first moment I knew I had been an *incarnate* part of the Noah energy.)

The coach we were travelling in stopped at the highest point of the plateau, some 4200 metres above sea level. I got out, still sensing how familiar it all was. The mountains were extremely calm and beautiful, stretching in every direction as far as the eye could see. I walked around, taking the scenery in, marvelling at the peacefulness. I was still feeling rather surprised because I had never had the smallest idea that Noah had incarnated in Peru. A little later, as I re-entered the coach, ready to continue the journey, a strange, unaccustomed fear enveloped my heart. I wondered what it was.

The coach set off at a good speed and, as we rounded the first corner, I let out a gasp. The whole area looked exactly as the image in my dream had done. I looked down the valley ahead of us and recognised the route the double-decker bus had taken. I knew beyond a shadow of a doubt that we were driving exactly where the arks had floated so long ago. I was still trying to come to terms with the fact that I had been an actual incarnate part of the Noah energy. I must have been a part of the energy that survived! The memories were so incredibly clear, almost as if they had happened yesterday.

As we drove on down between the mountains, I felt the ark had landed on dry ground some few hundred metres below the highest point. It would have been low ground at the time because the general sea level would have been much higher. I remembered we had settled there and started a new community from scratch.

A huge feeling of elation crept over me. At last, I knew for certain how my dream fitted into the picture and exactly what it meant. I asked if there was any confirmation I could have from source, and a short while later Ingrid spotted a sign by the road saying, 'Noah'. We had to laugh!

At the beginning of the day, I had remembered that my father at the time of the Split was absent from the scene of my death. He was a great golden lion who had walked beside me as an equal in previous incarnations. Dom was a part of that same energy at the time. As I continued to peruse this matter, while the coach continued on its way, the following truths dawned on me:

When Ingrid and I had arrived in Lima, we had met up with a third member of our group whom I shall call Leo. It took me a couple of days to see through Leo's front because he smoked constantly and this made me want to step away from him all the time. However, as there were only the three of us on the trip to start with, we could not be rude and we had to include him. As I managed to overcome my dislike of the smoke and spend more time with Leo, I realised he was a tremendously nice guy who had simply forgotten his roots.

As we approached the high plateaux in the mountains near Machu Picchu, I was reminded by Dom that Leo had been a lion during several lives before the Split and that I had known him very well. He had been my 'partner'. I could remember pacing the ground next to him, through the Machu Picchu mountain range, both of us moving calmly, firmly and majestically, side by side as equals, with a huge family pacing equally majestically behind us. We were well respected by the rest of the community and used only telepathic communication between ourselves, our family and those around us. We had walked together for many lifetimes in such a way. Sex was not physical at this stage of our evolution. Two souls connecting together as an energetic thought was enough to create a conception so that offspring could emerge. It was truly harmonious and what I reconnected with was probably what all of us are trying to reconnect with now, in our own ways. The 'oneness' communication between us was absolute. The peace, love, wisdom and joy were apparent and balanced in every fibre of our beings. I remembered bliss, but I also remembered I had not been conscious of the bliss at the time. I only knew it had been bliss as I reconnected with Leo in my current conscious state.

It was made apparent to me that Leo and I had made a pre-life agreement to re-join in Peru at this time and therefore had chosen the exact same holiday for the purpose. This enabled me to have a total reconnection with the pre-Split energy so I could reignite the memory of true union between male and female in a balanced way. It wasn't important for Leo to remember this right now, it was enough that he had brought himself to this point and allowed me to remember.

It was as these memories became clear that I felt the 'oneness' state recreate itself. I felt myself slip completely through the eye of the needle for the final time. I found myself floating around in the mountains, seeing the world exactly as it was in the pre-Split days. As I had one more week of the holiday to go at this point, I knew it would be enough time to pick up adequate energy and memories that I needed, in order to retain the pre-Split state when I returned home.

What a gift Leo had given me . . . and anyone who chose to connect with me in the future. Not only could I reconnect with the memory of how my own life had been before the Split but I was now ready to live it as a permanent state. This in turn would allow the energy of the pre-Split days to resonate throughout my body, throughout the farm and from there, to whoever wanted to connect with it.

Our coach arrived at a small Inca settlement called Raqchi. Here our guide showed us that part of the original Inca trail ran through the ruins. It was supposed to be the trail that was used by Inca pilgrims travelling from Lake Titicaca to Machu Picchu. Dom appeared at this point and informed me that this trail was actually far older than the Incas. It had in fact been used by people when the sea waters were very much higher. Young people and animals used to make the trek from the higher planes to Machu Picchu (the largest mountain in the area) as an important part of their life journey. The travellers could see Machu Picchu from many miles away and, when it was out of view, they travelled due south by the sun, thus keeping themselves on course. Having reached their destination, they would tarry a while and then re-trace their steps back to their own communities. When they finally reached their home again, they were considered the *wise ones.* He informed me I had made that pilgrimage on several occasions.

Machu Picchu, being by far the largest mountain within eye sight, seemed to the pre-Split people to be the central point of the world as they knew it. It therefore naturally drew life from all corners of South America, thus creating one of the strongest life-force energies of the times. The height and splendour of the mountain held a majestic significance for them. It was also surrounded by other great mountains, most of which still stand today. The highest at present stands at 5200 metres and is very close to the Machu Picchu site.

Tuning closely to the Inca path, I recalled that pilgrims of all descriptions had joined the path from all over the mountains. Small paths joined the main trail from everywhere. The feeling and visual memory I had of Machu Picchu towering over the rest of the mountain range was very powerful. As it had been considered the 'heart' of the earth plane at that time, it is interesting to note that Cusco is now the closest town to Machu Picchu and the original name of the town was Cosco, meaning 'of the heart'.

As we drove further down between the mountains, with the Inca trail running alongside us, we came to a divide where I knew the ancient trail I had followed so many lifetimes ago veered off to the left between two peaks. Everything in me wanted to turn left between those peaks but the modern road continued down through the valley and from then on the countryside became unfamiliar to me.

That night we stayed in Cusco, a smallish town nestling quietly in a tree-free basin surrounded by green-brown mountains. The most notable part of our stay there was when our guide told us that the flag for Cusco was a rainbow! I had asked the universe for confirmation of all that was happening and I was getting it.

Our guide also showed us the Cusco emblem that was roughly inscribed on the mountain side, just outside the city. I looked across at it from the mountain we were standing on. The emblem looked like the base of a boat in a U shape. Inside the 'U', there seemed to be a tall shape that looked like a double-decker bus. I felt as though I was looking directly at Noah's ark! It was only when I arrived back in England and saw a blown-up photo that I became aware of the details, as shown below:

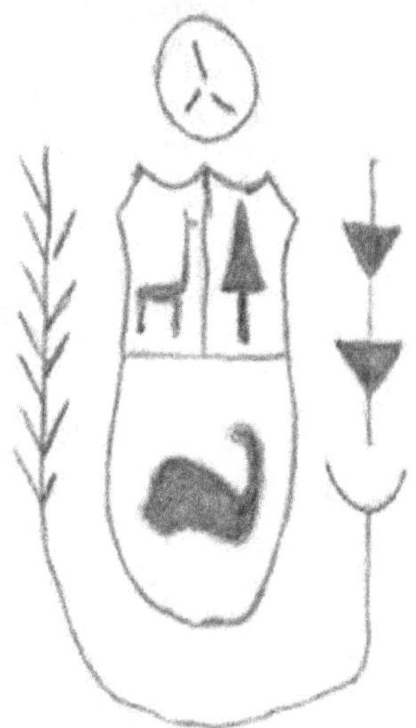

The Cusco Emblem

9

The Unusual Crystal

It was at about this time that I asked Dom what the exact significance of my journey to Machu Picchu was. He informed me that I was the bearer of an energetic key that would re-open the Machu Picchu site in order that the pre-Split energy could flow freely from the core out into the ether. I was a part of the 'healing' of the Split and I would help heal some of the carnage that the Split had left us with. From this one unconditional, conscious act, the pre-Split energy had the potential to spread worldwide, after bringing enlightenment back to an area that had suffered such 'apparent' darkness. Because I was choosing to do this consciously, I was knowingly and understandingly taking the pre-Split memory back where it belonged.

I think it's now about time I told you about the 'crystal' I have been aware of in my forehead.

A few years ago, I woke up in the middle of the night feeling there was a crystal inside the top section of my head.

It spread from my forehead to the back of my skull. It filled my brain area entirely.

As I lay in bed pondering this peculiar information, I realised the crystal was completely covered in dust. I licked the tip of my finger and psychically felt the dust on the crystal. The dust was stuck solid as if it had been there for aeons. I managed to scrape a little of the dust away and it became a little cleaner.

I didn't think too much about this incident for a while but, every few months, it would pop into my mind, at which time I would clean off a little more of the dust. I supposed everyone must carry a crystal in their brain and that we all take the dust off in our own good time.

About two years ago, I noticed the crystal was clean and that it was a beautiful, deep green-blue colour, like the ocean can be. It was clear and shining. I noted that this must be a good thing and it was progressing in the right direction. Gradually, during the following months, the crystal became a lighter and lighter shade until eventually it was completely translucent with a small aqua blue centre upon which it was pivoted. By now I was fascinated by its progress and started to mention it to a few interested parties.

One day, I was tuning in to the aqua blue centre and asked if this could become clear like the rest of the crystal. Immediately, the aqua blue disappeared, the crystal became translucent throughout and began to turn slowly on its axis.

For the whole of the summer of 2011, whenever I tuned in to it, the crystal turned slowly in my head. I felt it was picking up information for me and I simply supposed that we all carry a crystal in our heads which would be made known to us at some stage.

As Dom revealed the meaning of my journey to Machu Picchu, I suddenly felt the crystal become very heavy. My head felt heavy. I was told I must release the crystal energetically in a certain place in the centre of Machu Picchu. I would be told when and where and I wasn't to worry myself about it.

Apparently, I elected to carry this crystal back to the incarnated world at this time and by releasing it in a certain place on Machu Picchu on 3 November 2011, it would start to activate and spread its energy throughout the world.

The crystal felt so heavy by this stage that Dom took the weight for me and said he would hold it for me until I was ready to let it go. The weight then lifted and I felt better. Suddenly, Dom, quite randomly, announced to me: 'I am a messenger of light.' He was talking about himself!

The following morning, I awoke early to the sound of the sherpas making some tea. I felt that mum and Dom had stepped aside. Scanning around, I sensed an unfamiliar set of ancient energies around me. I asked who they were and was told they were mostly souls who had only incarnated once or twice on this planet while some of them had never incarnated on earth. They were energies that had been important at the time of the Split. The only two names I recognised were Elijah and Moses.

From this moment onwards, I knew that although our lovely Peruvian guide appeared to be in charge of this expedition, it was only on the physical plane. The ancient spirits (acting through me) were fully in charge on the spiritual plane. This was confirmed to me a few hours later when the duffle bags that we had to use for our trek were handed out. The one that was given to me had originally contained all the others. I was also given the weighing machine that would be used to weigh the duffle bags once we had packed them. Everyone had to come to my room to be weighed in. I was overjoyed to have such natural and simple signs of confirmation.

As I sank into a semi-trance state, I asked for the four days of the oncoming trek to unfold at the highest possible level. I felt the crystal begin revolving slightly faster. I felt it reach out to the world and I asked for the world's support for this mission. I also asked to be so highly tuned that I would do and say exactly as I should at all times.

The importance of the mission was building inside me. I had a feeling of nervous excitement and awe at what was about to happen. I felt worldwide spiritual excitement. Above all, I felt the approach of the healing of the Split at its deepest level.

10

The Trek to Machu Picchu

On Sunday 30 October, we awoke at 5.00 a.m., ready to start our journey. I felt inexplicably tearful, wishing that Dom was with me in the physical. However, I pulled myself together and after a short bus ride into the foothills of the relevant set of mountains, we arrived at the start of our trek. Full of nervous anticipation, we loaded our packs onto our backs and set off over a narrow wooden bridge and along a rough, stony track beside a river. We were bathed in warm, spring sunshine.

The scenery was beautiful as we climbed higher and higher. I was surprised there were so few trees around as I had intuitively expected a lot more. But the Andean mountain scenery was breath-taking and the air was so clean and fresh. We visited several Inca sites in various places as we came across them. Most of them were balanced precariously on cliff edges in the mountain's sides.

I felt increasingly tearful as we trekked on through the morning so eventually 'asked' why this was so. Dom told me he would have been walking with me if he had been alive. He had always intended to be with me on this exciting trek, to look after me and share the experience. He loved mountains as I do and his grief was doubling mine and showing itself through me. At this point, I really sobbed, but it was a good release for both of us.

Continuing up the steep, stony track, I still felt very, very sad. Why wasn't it leaving me? It then came to me that I was now feeling grief held within the land itself. I was picking up the grief, fear, shock, anger and loss that remained in the land from the 'dark days'. I felt it so acutely that I could not help but break out into deep sobs again. I asked for it to release through me.

At this point, Ingrid wondered what was going on and when I related my feelings to her, she stated that she had had a similar experience a year previously but she didn't know what it was. She came to understand her own experience through mine.

As the shock in the land was reverberating through me, I asked how I could possibly pass such an enormous emotion through my little body. It felt impossible to me! I was immediately told that once the crystal had been placed back where it belonged, it would start to turn slowly and draw the unwanted energies out of the land, people, vegetation and animals.

The massive weight of the emotions then left me abruptly and I felt Dom bouncing around me as he often does. He said he would be with me and Ingrid every step of the way to ensure we would be OK and that everything would happen as it should. He started to instruct us both as to how to achieve the steep climb ahead of us. It was wonderful to have him so 'present'. My energy began to return and I enjoyed the rest of that day.

At some point in the afternoon, I asked Dom if he could teach various members of the group important life lessons that they needed to learn. As mentioned before, one member of the group was the golden lion I had known many times before the Split and who had been my father at the actual time of the Split. Dom reminded me that he and Leo (the lion) were one and the same energy at the moment of the Split and that my asking for help for him would in fact help them both. This made much sense to me as I could see how they carried very similar traits. Leo also brought up many vivid memories for me because his presence constantly reminded me of the days before the Split. Therefore, I was re-experiencing this very important energy in a very tangible way. A little later on in the trip, it dawned on me that Dom, Leo and I must all be from the same soul group. Well, what a place for us all to meet!

On the Monday, I woke to a terrible nightmare during that first night in the mountains. Analysing it swiftly in my usual way, I became aware that it concerned the male/female imbalance on the planet. I pondered this imbalance during the 1000-metre climb we made the next day and, interestingly, I took a nasty fall, when I tripped and rolled several feet back down the mountain, near the summit of our climb. My balance was definitely struggling in an unusual manner. I felt the imbalance even more strongly as we descended into the cloudy valley to our second campsite. The energy at this point was very dark and I had great difficulty in overcoming my desire to run away.

Asking for an explanation, I remembered the terrible imbalance we created between male and female after the Split. Males, for the first time ever, were known to be physically bigger, stronger, more powerful and more dominating. Females seemed weaker, smaller and less important. Males took full advantage of their position at that time, as indeed some of them still do today. I felt this energy fully, as I roamed the campsite searching for answers. Indeed, one of the female members of the group was having a monthly period and this reminded me that it can be called 'the curse' because it was thought to be a divine curse at that time. Basically, men accused women of being cursed, and therefore they had to suffer the consequences of 'the curse', possibly because men believed in some respects that women were responsible for 'the darkness'.

As time went on, after the Split, the imbalance became greater and greater. Women felt their inferiority deeply, and men simply acted to strengthen that emotion. Indeed, sheer size and strength served to constantly prove the point. It is only now that the feminine is recognising itself and demanding equal rights that we are beginning to rebalance.

Ingrid and I had both met someone in the group we were travelling with whom we had known in other lifetimes and who greatly enhanced our journeys. The person I met was of course Leo. The interesting thing is that I had loved the person I met while the person she met had killed her. Therefore, the 'opposites' were again being highlighted. We both benefited in ways which, had these people not been there, could not have happened. The energy they represented was invaluable to both us and them. It is unlikely they will ever know what they did for us or realise on a personal level what we did for them, but it will be known by people like you.

At this point, I am going to share Ingrid's story with you. She very kindly allowed me to include it in these writings, for the benefit of all.

I came to be on a journey to Peru because something inside me said 'yes' when I was asked if I would like to go. The deeper implications and the level of healing Anna and I went through were extraordinary.

On the flight over, I said, 'We are going to heal the Split'. On one level, this sounds a bit grand and pseudo-spiritual but on a personal level, it was not so glamorous. It could have been anyone with a passion for adventure doing this trip, mixed with an inner listening, alertness and presence but the timing and synchronicities of other people's lives that met us on the trip were no accident. Part of my personal healing was connected with one of the members of the group who had subconsciously agreed to reconnect with me for a deep healing of past deeds. As memories and situations flooded back, I was able to forgive and send my compassion and healing for the highest good to a very troubled soul.

The whole picture of where I was at the time of the Split was not clear to me until I got to Peru. Her ancient land and ruins triggered old karmic memories that were pieced together with both Anna's and my insights. There were times on the Inca trail where I felt deep peace, joy, love and wisdom vibrating in all things. I responded to this sheer wildness and purity by singing and breathing in the timeless presence. I knew I had been in Peru before the time of the Split. I held a deep reconnection and recognition.

However, it was not all like this. Seeing deep chasms as my eye followed what seemed like geological cracks in the Andean mountains' contours evoked a memory of having fallen and died down one. I died with a huge sense of foreboding of things to come and I had not warned anybody. This set up resonance of a deep sense of shame, guilt and shock within me. It was imperative that I came back to redress my actions and also to return and share the knowledge I had before the time of the Split.

In the shock and chaos of the huge seismic upheaval, my spirit waited in limbo for a while until, out of my increasing urgency to return, I spontaneously jumped into the vacant body of a young girl who was caught up in witnessing scenes of massive destruction in a completely different time period. (This young girl had been so distressed by what she was witnessing that she had temporarily 'come out' of her body.) This part of my memory was powerfully awoken when Anna and I were on Tequila Island in the middle of Lake Titicaca. I had dreamt of a particular gateway on the island about six months before our trip. And here I was! And here the gateway was! In the dream, I had witnessed chaos and mayhem of bodies strewn everywhere. I feared for my life as I watched the fighting and massacre. As Anna and I walked the very same pathway, I remembered that the young girl's father had been looking for her. He was hugely relieved to find she was alive, grabbed her by the arm and took her to safety. She did not recognise her father because she was not the same spirit of the little girl he had known.

Often in this lifetime, I have felt I do not belong, but picking up the threads of this story, I have made connections to my current life and emotional and mental bodies that now make so much more sense. I reincarnated many times in that era, to try and redress the balance, but it was not possible to do so then, as there was too much darkness, chaos and upheaval.

A further time of 'karmic recall' that happened after the Split was brought to my attention due to my menses time. During these dark times, I was able to remember and heal a fatal karmic life. My excessive pre-menopausal bleeding, through a series of events, took me to a healing that touched the core of me. The situation itself was simply because someone was laughing at me in my plight. This was small in itself but my reaction of anger was huge. It triggered the laugh in the past that had condemned me for being a woman, innocent and bleeding. I had died at the point of a sword. I had been made an example of, made a mockery of and I had been tortured and mutilated for having the 'curse'. My executioner was a member of our group. It was his laugh that made my skin crawl. The power of forgiveness works on so many levels. It could have been any woman experiencing deep archetypal feminine wounding and humiliation. Yet symbolically, my return to Peru after many aeons somehow made it possible for the healing of the feminine, on many levels, to go so much deeper.

Looking back, I realise that part of my purpose in returning to Peru was to redress the imbalance of the masculine and the feminine that is tangibly felt around the Inca ruins. This happened primarily because I addressed a huge aspect of my own feminine wounding. I returned to Peru so that womankind could now be honoured and the blood of the earth flow pure; that woman should walk beside man, not behind, as was witnessed on the islands of Lake Titicaca.

It is important to remember that Machu Picchu was of course patriarchal. Our guide told us that the Inca leader would have a hundred concubines and, after he had finished with them, they would be shared out among his army of men. Throughout the trip, we had seen stone blocks that had been used for blood sacrifices of virgins to the sun god. These had left me with a haunted feeling. So maybe it was no surprise that I shed my blood and had to heal deep humiliation and torture. I was able to release the emotional trauma and memory from these times and heal, on a profound level, 'the Split in me'. My insight that we had come to heal the Split had first to catapult me into my own healing journey before it could address the bigger picture.

My personal healing came as I forgave the person who had caused me so much pain. Anna then asked me if I was willing to give my life to God. After some thought, I said I was willing to surrender my life fully to the divine light. I have surrendered my life many times but with an agenda of different healing modalities. This time I was being asked to serve in any way that the universe chose. I was also being asked to go through the eye of the needle and I said, 'yes'. A vast energetic vibration of the highest light and love poured through me. I felt this expand from me into the room. I felt space and light everywhere moving outwards. I did not know what this meant for the future. I only *knew* I would be guided by the still small voice within.

I am truly grateful.

After an uncomfortable night, I rose very early and decided to climb up both sides of the valley we were camping in. One side was dark and damp and felt very sad. The other side was lighter and I could see that the sun might reach it soon. I sat on a boulder on the darker side and sensed some of the ancient atrocities that had taken place in the cloud valley surrounding me. As I merged myself fully into the dark days of the Split, I was so glad I had not consciously done this the night before. It made me feel like I never wanted to go back down to the campsite. The atrocities that had taken place there were beyond words. I asked for all the energy from those times to be released and for the male/female balance to be fully restored. I then asked for this release to spread throughout the world.

When I finally came back into my body, I realised the sun was drawing much closer and would soon be shining on the other side of the valley. I quickly made my way over to the lighter side and sat down on a small rock to watch the dawn appearing. The sky was becoming a true, clear blue and I felt healing coming to the area. I knew it would fill the valley before I left. I asked for all future visitors to feel the deep healing between male and female when they visited the valley, knowing the perfect sunshine was the full recognition of the healing that had taken place that morning. I pondered that the male/female balance within our group was nine male to five female. I laughingly mused that the females were actually not outdone in terms of ability or noise level. Therefore, the group energy was probably quite evenly balanced.

The sun was shining fully on me by now. I watched the other visiting groups pack up their camps and realised, thankfully, that our group leader was going to take us out of the valley last. He had unconsciously given me time to receive all this information and still return to the campsite on time. I took in a deep breath and forced myself back down to the campsite. As I did so, I asked for the light within me to release and fill/heal the area. My action would bring conscious light (release) back in to the scene of devastation I had previously tuned in to.

A little later, as I walked back out of the campsite, which was now bathed in beautiful sunshine, I felt I was pulling all the 'yuck' out of the valley with me. I felt as if I was pulling out some type of plug. My own body felt full of yuck too, so, as I climbed, I quickly let it out into the ether and continued clearing it thoroughly as I made the steep ascent away from the scene.

The walk that day was the most beautiful of all. The scenery gradually altered and became greener. Trees became more and more numerous and larger. The vegetation around was lush and the wildlife was abundant. Beautiful birds sang and chirped happily as we walked along. I recognised this area was close to where I had actually lived at the time of the Split. We progressed deeper into the jungle and it was rapidly becoming exactly as I had expected. I also noted with surprise that the scenery exactly matched so many of the scenes I have had opened up to me by so many people when they have shared their moment of the Split. I felt elated. I recognised everything from the steep cliff drops to the jungle-filled landscape. It made me realise just how many people who had come to me in the last two years had been in Peru at the time of the Split. It also confirmed the accuracy of what I had been doing. I gasped repeatedly as memory after memory unfolded. It was truly a wonderful experience that reconnected me with my past.

Our campsite that evening was high in the mountain range and therefore held a much better atmosphere than the previous one had, for which I was very thankful. The clouds were gathering in the valley below us so we couldn't see much but there was an interesting Inca site to explore nearby. We were surrounded by wonderful, brightly coloured birds, and alpacas roamed freely over the Inca ruins. I felt moved to ask the light to come from the core and heal all of us from the time of the Split through to the present, to the greatest degree possible.

The final day of the trek dawned and I took myself off on one of my early morning walks again. I did this mainly to warm up after another cold, sleepless night. As I walked along, I felt an unaccountable anger towards Leo. He had made me quite angry the night before but I thought I had put that incident behind me. However, I recalled the anger and a sense that he had not been *there* for me the evening before. Then I remembered he had not been *there* for me at the time of the Split. And, to my surprise, I burst into tears as I remembered that my father had not been *there* for me in this life. After a good sob, I reasoned that it had never mattered to me that my father had not been there for me, so why was I upset about it now? I then realised it represented a final part of my personal rebalancing process that was coming into my consciousness so I could fully heal.

I made my way back to the camp feeling quite apprehensive about what might happen that day. As I walked, I again felt heavy energy and deep sadness from the time of the Split. It was all-encompassing. I couldn't think what I could do about it so I simply opened myself up and asked for help. I suddenly felt that by doing this I would also be opening up my psychic abilities to a much greater degree. Sure enough, shortly afterwards, I felt the familiar boundaries I had held receding and the sadness lifting. I felt in perfect balance. I felt the peace, love, wisdom, harmony, and indeed the joy that had been missing for so long, returning to my heart.

The downhill stretch for that morning was quite testing. I knew we were very close to Machu Picchu but, as yet, we could see nothing of it. I could feel an increase in tension within me but I plodded on, trusting that all that was needed would be perfectly provided. We stopped six kilometres away from our destination for lunch. I told Ingrid that, during the afternoon, I wanted to bring up the rear of the group in order to fully receive all that I needed to receive. She agreed to accompany me.

Three kilometres from the sun gate (the entrance to Machu Picchu), I started to go into a trance state. From that moment, I began to pick up truths from the time of the Split and they came as follows:

The first experience I had was of feeling some falling, molten rocks crashing down on me from above. I felt thick heat energy and had a powerful feeling of shock and fear. I realised the mountain itself was giving off these vibes. I was aware that the people, animals and vegetation where I was walking had experienced falling lava and had been killed by it. They had no knowledge of why or what was happening. It all happened too quickly for them. I could sense the mountain was full of anger so I asked it why. Immediately, I felt the push from the core of the planet, just as I had done so long ago when Dom first related the revelations to me. I felt a yearning from the light energy to know itself, coming from the core and pushing outwards and upwards. The yearning emotion collected in a massive heap beneath the Machu Picchu mountain. The push eventually became so strong that it channelled a path up through the centre of the mountain and shot high into the sky for many hundreds of metres. I saw an orange-red stream of fire heading skyward, out of control.

(It might be worth mentioning here that my husband in this life was a part of the Machu Picchu Mountain energy at this very moment. What I had not known before was that many of the creatures that survived the volcanic eruptions started to blame the mountain for what had happened. So just before the split the mountain had been a trusty place of refuge, a sacred site and then suddenly it seemed to have let everyone down and fingers were pointed, so to speak. Much of the surviving life could not see beyond the fact that the explosions from the mountain had seemingly changed their lives.)

Who do you know that carries this volcanic energy? For we who pointed fingers at that time must surely ask for forgiveness for blaming the mountain so that the energy may heal.

By this time, we were experiencing our first really heavy rain of the holiday. Realising it was significant, I asked what it meant. Apparently, the column of fire had gone straight through the clouds and scattered them wildly all over the sky. Everything in the air went into a panic as it 'experienced' for the first time. The reaction sent an enormous cloud burst or storm over the entire area.

The rain lessened and we walked on, feeling the devastation as everything in the area was being killed by the shifting ground and the falling lava. The energy around us held mainly panic, confusion, shock and untold levels of fear.

At this point, Ingrid suddenly asked me about the significance of crystals. I, in turn, asked the mountain. Apparently, at the time of the Split, the peak of the mountain was pure, clear crystal. It was an area that had not been touched by any human, animal or type of vegetation. When the volcano erupted, it blew the top of the mountain into the sky from where it divided into millions of pieces. As the planet was also going through a major shift or spin at the same time, it spread the crystal far and wide into the atmosphere and it took a long time for all the pieces to fall back to earth.

The true meaning of crystal is 'pure rock'. The energy it holds is 'memory'. It is the memory of peace, wisdom, love and joy that was held in perfect balance before the Split. Nowadays, a large piece of crystal can still hold enough untouched memory within it to retain its original power. This is the only true power of any crystal.

As we walked on, a group of about nine people passed us. I was told that these nine people had each answered the call to come back to the mountain. They had all been at Machu Picchu at the time of the Split and had returned together to help the mountain heal. It was important for them to walk as a group for it was only 'as a group' that their energy could remember itself. I then saw a solitary man go by. He carried an angry energy, though I don't suppose he knew it. Suddenly, I knew that nearly everyone on the mountain that day had come to bring back an original memory that had been lost at the time of the Split. They had all answered a deep call and were part of the universal plan to heal the Split. This included our own group that we had been travelling with. Our group was half light energy and half dark. It was in perfect balance.

I felt a change in my body. I knew Ingrid and I must now free our 'selves' from the mountain's story and allow the love and light, peace and healing that usually flows through us, to flow into the mountain. I suggested we 'drive' it into the mountain as we walked, seeing it go right through the mountain. Just after I said this, we rounded a corner and saw a flight of rough stone steps ahead of us. Was this the sun gate? We didn't know. However, we climbed the steps, sending deep shafts of healing through the mountain as we did so. At the top, there seemed to be no one around. But, as we stepped through the gateway, there was a dramatic change in the energy. It was one of the most dramatic changes either of us has ever felt. The next two steps told me that we were now walking *inside* the original mountain, as it had been before the volcanic eruption at the time of the Split. I walked on in a complete daze!

Understanding that we were now walking *inside* the original mountain, it became obvious that the high bank to our left was the inside of the old original exterior! The clear space to our right was the hole left by the original explosion. In the distance to the right was a half-moon shape of high peaks that had obviously been the outer edge of the original mountain. The atmosphere was truly breath-taking—so calm, so untouched, so pure and so intense. There was no one in sight.

We strolled on, gasping in amazement. It was obvious we were in a huge void that had been left by the explosion all those years ago. We felt like tiptoeing through, as if we had found a huge secret that no one else knew about. Eventually, we came to the real sun gate/entrance. The other group members were waiting for us excitedly, thrilled to have made it there. Ingrid and I climbed the stone stairs but unfortunately there was little to view from the top. The intermittent cloud of the day took everything away, leaving us with fog and a distant impression of the other half of our 'bowl'.

However, I was experiencing *all* that mattered to the universe. Looking across to the 'Lost City of the Incas' that had been built within the Machu Picchu mountain, I knew the original mountain had covered the entire massive area at one time. The rock that the sun gate was built on was not central to the site but I could see a smaller peak in the distance that probably was. The clouds cleared momentarily and we could see the Inca ruins through the fog. I briefly wondered where we were to place 'the memory'.

After waiting for some time for the fog to clear, our guide led us along the inside of the old outside wall (if you see what I mean). To everyone else, we were simply approaching the Inca city along a narrow path. As we walked, I realised just how big the original mountain had been, possibly close to the size of Everest, which stands at just under 9000 metres.

At this point, Ingrid asked me: what was the purpose of placing the crystal? I was able to explain that the crystal was only a memory. I was consciously carrying as much memory as I could back to the heart of the mountain and reminding it of the pre-Split days. I was also reminding it of what had happened during the Split and in doing so was bringing it healing which would spread throughout the world in due course. Because Machu Picchu was one of the hardest hit areas on our planet at the time of the Split (possibly *the* hardest hit), it would be one of the most important areas to heal in order to bring about the change we are all hoping for.

As we walked towards the Inca city in the centre of the Machu Picchu bowl, I intuitively picked out a couple of places that the crystal might be left. One was in the bottom of a valley above a river, where I felt the energy spiralling upwards and the other was on the top of a small nearby peak that I judged was fairly central. This peak had a rainbow flag on top of it. I asked for guidance as to which place would be best.

A little later, when I was briefly alone, I looked across at the peak. To my astonishment, there was a real rainbow coming out from its centre, reaching upwards towards the sky. I knew in an instant I had been given a sign. Ingrid was about a hundred metres below me but she too saw the rainbow (it was the only rainbow we saw the whole time we were on the site) and she also knew it was our sign. However, we knew we were not to place the crystal until the following day so we spent the rest of the afternoon admiring the views in the patchy sunlight.

At one point, I felt the need to shout silently to the interior of the original mountain: 'Remember who you are. Remember what you have been. It's time now to re-awaken and become the balance that you once were.' I felt my silent voice reverberate around the peaks, hitting each one of them in turn and echoing back to each other as they heard the message.

On the journey back to the hotel that night, I was wondering why I had been entrusted to bring the 'memory' back home! I knew I was a very ordinary person with no special connections. Dom then told me that there were very few souls who had remained relatively untainted after the Split and still had the capacity to remember. Ordinary was good! There was enough purity within me to qualify for the job. I had apparently applied and been accepted!

11

A Day Never to Be Forgotten

Early on 3 November 2011, we set off in the pouring rain for a full tour of the Machu Picchu city. Everyone in our group was miserable and hoping for the sun to come through but the forecast was bleak. We all bought ponchos and boarded the bus, as well prepared as we could be for what lay ahead.

Our guide was to give us a two-and-a-half-hour tour of the main buildings on the site, after which we were free to do as we wished for a few hours. Ingrid and I decided to follow the tour and then see what the universe asked of us after that.

We listened for an in-depth half hour, during which we learnt about the American who had discovered the Lost City of the Incas exactly 100 years previously. When he found it, it had been covered with trees and was therefore invisible to most people. He was apparently convinced there was gold hidden somewhere and so he searched high and low throughout the site but to no avail. I privately thought to myself: 'Well, you were right, there was gold to be found. But not the sort you were expecting!'

After that, we walked along the path to a place where two well-preserved walls were running parallel across the entire site. They were about 3 feet tall and about 6 feet apart. The walls ran in a dead straight line, down into the base of the site, through the spiral of energy I had felt earlier and across to the peak where I had felt we should leave the memory.

Our guide told us that the Incas had not built anything between those two walls because they felt there had been a massive tectonic plate movement at some stage in history and the ground wasn't safe. He pointed to 'my' chosen peak and said the fault line had extended through it and well beyond it. Although I thought I heard what the guide said the first time, my ears could hardly take in his words. In an awed whisper, I said to the guide, 'Can you say that again, please?' He patiently did. And I think the whole site revolved at least twice in front of my eyes.

I realised with the most incredible surprise I could ever experience that I was actually looking at the physical manifestation of the Split.

The tectonic plates had caused a shift right through the heart of the Machu Picchu mountain and had helped bring about its collapse. The volcanic eruption that had occurred would have been in the direct line of the plate movement, and the peak I intended to put the memory back onto was directly behind that. In that moment, I knew beyond a shadow of a doubt that all the information from

Dom was unbelievably accurate. Everything he had told me was indeed proved to me here. I had never expected such confirmation. I had never expected to *see* the physical manifestation of the Split!

After that, I hardly heard a word our guide said. I simply waited and, once free of our tour, I tried to 'clear' myself fully so I would be ready for the job I had to do. It was extremely difficult in the pouring rain and with all the tourists about. However, finding a little shelter beside a high wall, I realised the tourists had now started to leave the mountain as the rain fell even faster. A feeling of amusement spread over me. The rain was clearing the mountain for me so I could do my job with the least interruption possible! Pretty soon, I felt my clarity return and immediately sensed I should walk the length of the Split between the walls even though it was not officially allowed.

I dropped down over the edge of the wall and slowly made my way down its length. As I did so, I felt the memory spreading all over the site. I was somehow letting it go. I stopped half way and allowed my story to unfold within the Split. I felt two periods of time coming together: the pre-Split days to my left and the post-Split days to my right. Somehow they seemed to merge where I was standing. I continued slowly between the walls, feeling the merging and healing continue, until I reached a large stone near the base of the site. There I stopped again and let my gaze run to the top of the peak where we had seen the rainbow the day before. I felt the crystal/memory lift from me. I saw it come to rest near the flag. I asked it to heal the Split and to send its healing energy all over the world. I felt as if I was inserting my small piece of the jigsaw into the bigger picture!

I then experienced *life* from inside the Split. I experienced a peace that was so pure and deep I did not want to move. I felt a unity I had never felt before. I saw two golden lions pacing side by side down the Split. One was my golden lion friend, Leo, and one was me. Behind us was our stream of cubs, all pacing with equal pride. We lions had a gentle, loving, wise, caring and deeply peaceful air about us. I recognised the unity, trust and equality that we knew before the Split occurred. I knew that female and male were as one. I knew that one day our world would return to this state, consciously, and we would all re-experience our true heritage once more.

Since returning home, I occasionally tune in to the crystal to see how it is doing. At first, it turned slowly, gathering itself in its new/old position. After a few days, it began to sparkle and shine. Now it is glowing from the top of the mountain. It shines like a crown, and I trust it is doing what I asked it to do!

12

What the Future Holds

The following revelations began when I was watching Professor Brian Cox's programme, *The Wonders of the Universe*, on television (BBC, 2011b). He was talking about gravity and, as he talked, I realised his explanation matched exactly the one I was given during Dom's revelations, only he was using scientific terms. I also realised my spiritual explanations answered questions that scientists could not answer at that time.

When Professor Cox started to talk about the galaxy and the black hole in the centre of the Milky Way, he could only take the explanation so far and then stated that when they got to the centre of the black hole, they 'lost the link' and as yet science could take the explanation no further. I realised that I could! I realised the black hole was an illusion, the same illusion as 'black' on this planet. The difference is of course that the illusion of the black hole in the Milky Way has apparently 'won' and now swallows up anything light that goes into it. (Professor Cox had said on the programme, 'Not even the light can survive'.)

I began to see the universal significance of this planet's role in our galaxy. What we, as a planet, are going through could carry implications far beyond this world. If we can achieve becoming light again consciously and *choose* to overcome the 'black' by free will, we can then, as a collective, potentially go on and defeat all the black holes in the cosmos.

No wonder the rest of the star-lit or planet-filled space is watching us so intently at this moment. Its future partially depends on our success! And yes! We are getting there.

A few weeks later, after one of the monthly meetings at the retreat, we all shared the difficulty of understanding the significance of 2012 and wondered why so many of us were feeling *rushed, bewildered, uncertain, excited, awed, overwhelmed, as if we were nearly there, a sense of momentum building, a deep sense of knowing*, etc. The conversation threw everything up in the air for me, so I asked source to rearrange it for me in a way I could understand. I received the following explanation:

Just before the time of the Split, there were some wise incarnated souls who felt a change approaching. They didn't know what they were feeling, but they felt an uncertainty and an apprehension. When the Split came, they tried to hold on to their wisdoms and truths but each was eventually swamped, by what appeared to be a greater force than they understood. Thus, the incarnated part of the planet submerged fully into the illusion of the 'dark days'.

There are, similarly, wise souls incarnated at present who feel the same uncertainty and are apprehensive about what is happening now. Many are trying to explain this, creating all manner of stories, hence the conversation at our Sunday meeting was a mix of some very bizarre ideas and some very sound ones.

I only speak a truth when it has been given to me from source. Going to source with all these complex thoughts and handing them over completely allowed source to reshuffle them for me and feed back the truth.

We are currently going through a state of rebalancing. There is at last enough incarnated 'light' to allow a further transition on our planet and this is causing a massive re-shift, giving a greater portion of the balance back to the light once more. The planet has (of its own free will) become light enough to take it from its current precarious position (which it has held since the Split) to a rather more stable one. This happened early in 2013 when the planetary alignment was in an excellent position to benefit. The feeling of being rushed was present because 'those in the know' realised, and have always realised, that if we could rebalance and transform exactly when this planetary alignment happened, the beneficial ripple effect on the rest of the universe would be maximised.

It is not that the rest of the universe is *making* us achieve all this. It is rather that *we* are achieving it of our own free will. *We are choosing to become selfless and go back to the light.* We are letting go of the illusion of our own greatness/self that the first moments of consciousness gave us, and realising we could become so much happier as 'conscious beings of light'.

We can *ask* for help from other light sources on other planets and they will give it. But they cannot give it to us unless we ask. Something 'out there' is not engineering our future . . . we are! The rest of the cosmos will benefit in untold measure as our planet succeeds of its own free will. They are watching us closely, they are *willing* us to do it at this time, so they can benefit to the greatest extent.

What is happening is of momentous importance to the whole complex system of creation. At the very moment that enough incarnated matter, whether human, animal, plant or rock, became light enough, success was assured for our planetary shift. At that very moment, the 'darkness' was forced to lessen its grip. The transparency that the spiritual world currently experiences is now becoming apparent enough on earth to force darkness/illusion to examine itself, whether it wants to or not. There are less and less places to hide. The light beings that have helped to create this are now able to fully ascend and become transparent beings of love in the incarnated world. In other words, they can become fully conscious beings. Heaven is starting to emerge on earth. The darkest parts of our planet are becoming visible to us all and, in the shame of this moment, they are either choosing to pass on or change. If they pass on, they will still have to undergo a further reincarnation if they wish to become a conscious part of this wonderful process. If they choose to stay, they have the chance to become lighter in this incarnation.

Every living thing is, at this very moment of the shift, accountable for itself. To the degree in which each part of creation has worked on becoming lighter, it is moving through into the new era. Change is inevitable for survival. The critical mass will have its way. As we, the peoples of this earth, bring this moment to fruition, the experiment that is earth is achieving its purpose and it will have far-reaching effects way beyond our wildest dreams.

Those who set the predictions for these events are ourselves. We predicted this event because there was a part of us that knew our purpose. The predictions set the intention. We are now at the climax of that intention.

The conscious duality that is ours, once fully conquered, will remain in the ether forever—it can never be undone. Our energy can transfer to other planets to a greater or lesser degree as they approach us. The enlightening ripples emanating from earth will affect the entire cosmos, thus ensuring our success spreads throughout the galaxies forever.

View of Machu Picchu, clearly showing the split running across the base of the picture

Afterword

The *memories* around the time of the Split that have been related in this book are coming back to human consciousness now because we are going through a further shift. We need to understand who we have been and what we have been through in order to remember who we are.

The enlightenment journey is becoming increasingly testing. As we enlighten, it becomes more and more difficult to tolerate the 'darkness' around us. After returning from Peru, having experienced the amazing pre-Split energy for nearly two weeks, the plunge back into my usual life was almost unbearable. I had asked for the pre-Split energy to remain in me, around me and throughout the farm, which was a lovely idea, but the reality was that the energy was so far removed from the rest of the world that the gulf that opened up felt nearly unbridgeable. I felt as if I was on a second double-decker bus ride and I must hang on to the hand rail, trusting my intuition, until the second bus could find dry land.

I did not know what my personal *tomorrow* would bring. I only knew that the peace and joy within me had reached its highest level yet and was worth striving for. I had to hang on. I would hang on. I so firmly believed we would know peace throughout the world before too long.

However, twelve months later, having gone through the massive enlightenment process during the Winter of 2012/2013 I can now explain this a little differently.

I no longer feel the gap is unbridgeable. I *am* the true light. What is around me is also the light. The difficulties I was experiencing when I came back from Peru are diminishing. I glow from where I am, on anything that chooses to come into my space. I long for the world to remember the joy of 'being' as I do within, and l long for what is without to join me.

Some enlightening souls are choosing to pass over. My plea to you as you enlighten is to stay here and trust, just as we managed to remain in the days of Noah. We need many enlightened beings to be incarnate. We need to bring the highest level of consciousness that we can into the physical state. I rejoice for all those souls who are standing up to their leaders all over the world. They do not want to tolerate the imbalance on our planet any longer. They will bring change, as we will—if we can just hang on. The choice is ours.

I am glad Dom and I have completed these words and that we now have the opportunity to share them with you. It has been a relentless task for the last few years and I am relieved not to have to continually re-live 'our' very painful story. I have managed to move on.

However, I do not regret the understandings the pain has brought me, the huge personal healing and the increased ability to help other people in a deeper and better way.

If you, in return, could pass these writings on, wherever you feel it would be appropriate, we will all be serving the greater good, in the highest possible way.

Further copies of this book and my first book, *From Chrysalis to Butterfly* (2008), can be obtained from Amazon.co.uk, from the publishers or directly from me at www.cotswoldhealingretreat.co.uk

Be the light.

Spread the light.

Share your light.

We are one

Appendix 1
Some Extras from Dom

The following are some interesting episodes that have taken place between Dom and I that people have found useful, and therefore I have included them in these writings.

The apple

Dom has shown me that our planet can be likened to an apple. When you look at an apple and you see it in all its glory, it is round, colourful, shiny, wholesome, etc. If you imagine all the air and the water taken out of the apple, it would shrivel to less than half the size. Likewise, if you were to suck the 'spiritual' out of the world we live in, it would become less than half the size.

Spiritual and physical co-habitate to form our planet as we know it, as do the water and matter which form the apple.

Actually, it's an interesting thought that perhaps the earth literally expanded as the light energy pushed its way to the surface and exploded. Maybe it really was originally half or even quarter of the size it is now!

Windows

During the first few days after Dom passed over, he showed himself to me by waving from one of the house windows. Then, in a fleeting second, he appeared in all the house windows, one after the other. I heard him say, 'Look mum! Look how fast I can move now!!' I shrieked with laughter. It was so typical of him to share something like that.

Another joke

One day, I was walking between the Cedar of Lebanon and the beech tree in my garden and I could feel Dom and my mum in the beech tree. I said to Dom: 'Dom, why are you always in the beech tree and not in the cedar?' He replied, 'Gran can't climb the cedar!'

The cedar tree has an enormous fat trunk which no one can climb easily! Dom used to climb it with ropes but, to my knowledge, my mum had never been up it. I just loved his sense of humour and I loved the natural way in which he referred to my mum as 'Gran'.

Communication

The normal way in which Dom speaks to me when he is around is testimony to the fact that he lives in exactly the same way now as he did when he was in his body. The only difference is that I can't physically see him. He does, however, slide around his life line and isn't always in his 'last life' mode. Sometimes I feel him as I knew him in this life but, at other times, although I know it's him, where he is speaking from is not necessarily a place that I know. By speaking to me from different planes, he can expand my knowledge in countless helpful ways. He often helps me, from an unknown plane, to help people who come to see me. He needs to, in order to help that person for the best. He is learning to help people in a better and better way, and if he doesn't know the answer to a question straight away I feel him shoot off (just as he used to in this life) to get the answer.

More recently, Dom has been communicating from what one might call an even broader space. Apparently, because I was asking for deeper insight into the time before this planet began, he has shot off into that and communicates to me from there. So, sometimes when I feel him, it is not in a personal way but in a 'general' way. But I still know it's him. Also, because I am constantly pursuing spiritual knowledge and asking him to help me, Dom is able to grow on the other side in a way he would not be able to, if I didn't ask him questions.

More about general balance

We are *so* expendable. As long as we are of use to 'the evolutionary process', in other words, on the *right* side of our pivot point, our lives have a true purpose. We become expendable when we function on the wrong side of our pivot point, and we fail to learn our lessons through stubbornness or fear. The universe itself actually doesn't care. If we die, we are simply moving on or changing plane to a position where we *can* be useful. The bigger picture doesn't evaluate things like we do. All this desire to save a life at all costs is of minor relevance. However, it must be said that the universe will use every situation we give it to the best advantage it can, though the most important 'reason for being' is to enlighten as much as possible as we live each life.

Asking to be balanced at every level is a hugely important prayer we can offer and it is currently not used enough. If we ask to be balanced, we will always be moving towards 'growth'. If we sit ignorantly imbalanced, we are in danger of becoming vulnerable. Just knowing this will change our lives. Knowing it at as deep a level as possible is also something to ask for. This is such a huge gift of understanding that Dom has selflessly brought us.

Also understand that balance runs through the centre of every part of existence. A cake has to be made with carefully balanced ingredients in order to give the best result. A business has to be balanced in order to expand and flourish. As individuals, we need to be balanced in order to grow safely. The world needs to be finely balanced in order to succeed in its mission. The cosmos has to be balanced as it pursues its quest to know itself.

Now is the time to fine-tune our balance at every level. Wherever we are or whoever we are, we each have different pivot points relevant to ourselves. We can only work from our own pivot point, not from anyone else's.

One great certainty that has solidified in me since receiving the revelations is the deep and positive knowledge that there is nothing *new* about any of this. It is *all* a part of our current progress. It has always been part of it and it always will be.

My holiday

During August 2010, I had a particularly busy week at the retreat. A lot of people were coming and going and I was cooking lunch for an elderly guest every day. I had one guest who I needed to be constantly tuned in to, I had my other guests' needs to attend to and I was exhausted.

A friend offered to come and look after *me* for a couple of days to allow me to take a break from the daily chores in my own house! This sounded like a wonderful idea and I was just about to work out how this could be accomplished when an astonishing thing happened.

I was walking through the 'magic woods' where all my other revelations have taken place when I felt Dom join me. I was delighted as I had not felt him so vividly for a long time.

First, he told me that if he had been alive, we would have been going on a holiday to the Swiss Alps together.

I mentioned that we had planned to do this the previous year (a year after he died) but he simply said, 'It wouldn't have happened then, mum! We would have gone at this time instead'. I didn't disbelieve him. Things are regularly changing in our family's plans.

As I walked along, I started to recall the holiday we had already had together in the Swiss Alps, the year before he died. It was such a wonderful memory that I often thought back to it, sometimes very tearfully and sometimes very happily. On this occasion, I had not been thinking about it for very long before I realised Dom was trying to tell me that this experience was different.

He said, 'Come with me, mum!'

I wasn't sure what he meant but I felt he was surrounding me and taking me to the Alps. Suddenly, we seemed to be at the top of a mountain looking down at a village below us. I went back into my memory and remembered the beautiful views we had seen on our holiday. Dom was communicating that this was a different view. I looked again and saw that it was!

He said, 'Do you want to slide down the mountain on your bum?'

I said, 'We will bump into poles and pine trees and things.'

Dom replied, 'No mum! Just slide and trust! You don't need to worry about hitting things in my world. You just trust you will be safe and *you will be* safe.'

The next instant, I felt myself sliding down the mountain. The wind was loud in my ears and the sensation of sliding really fast was exhilarating. All too soon I reached the bottom.

Dom and I found ourselves on the outskirts of a pretty village. We walked along a narrow, snow-covered lane, towards the centre. I glimpsed a carpenter's shop with simply designed wooden benches outside the door. At this point, I slipped back into memory and remembered some of the shops we had seen on our first holiday together. Dom gently got my attention.

'Mum! Your first thought was correct. We are walking past a carpenter's shop!'

I managed to let go of the memory and slip back next to Dom on our new holiday. We passed a tiny bakery and I saw and smelt all the fresh croissants and bread in the window. Smelling them and just being aware of the baker's shop seemed to be enough.

I asked Dom, 'Is this how it is for you? Do you simply walk past and go through the sensations?'

He replied, 'Yes, exactly that! And you can have the sensations to the highest degree possible. Isn't it wonderful?'

And I had to agree that it was my finest ever experience of walking past a bakery.

Next, Dom asked if I would like to go to the top of the mountain that we could see ahead of us. I looked consideringly at it, wondering for a fleeting second if I could make it to the top at Dom's pace.

He said, 'It's OK, mum. Just relax into it and we'll go together.'

I suddenly found myself engulfed in a rush of air and ascending rapidly up the mountain side. We travelled so fast that we seemed to be at the top in no time. The mountain summit was covered in snow. I looked about me and, once again, slipped back into 'normal' memory of a skiing holiday that the family had once had. Dom gently nudged me back and I saw again the view that was really ahead of me. A scene that was completely new to me was in front of my eyes. It was simply beautiful: snow-capped peaks and tree-filled valleys as far as the eye could see.

Dom asked, 'Would you like to ski down, mum?'

'I'm not a good enough skier', I replied.

'Just imagine the best skier that you have ever seen and that is who you will be', came Dom's response.

I imagined a professional skier I had once seen on television. The next thing I knew I was skiing rapidly down a very steep slope, twisting and turning, cornering and sliding, wind rushing through my hair and past my face, leaving me feeling absolutely exhilarated. I didn't want it to end.

Dom took me next to the peak of a very high mountain. Just as we approached the top, I said to Dom,

'We can't go to the top of this one. It's too foggy.'

Indeed, we couldn't see the top. It was wrapped in a complete blanket of thick cloud. Dom said to me,

'This is the best bit of all, mum. This is one of the few times in my world when I can be completely alone. No one can see me unless they happen to pass by and enter the cloud. You and I can be relatively alone and it is one of the only ways on my side that we can have some degree of privacy.'

I was amazed—the story of Moses came into my mind and I resolved to look it up when I got home.

Dom asked if I would like a ride on a cloud. He found us a small one and we sat with our feet dangling over the edge. Our cloud took us gently over the beautiful mountains and valleys. By this time, I had completely stopped fighting the experience and I sat contentedly watching the scenery go by. The sun shone on our backs, gently warming us and casting its glow over the mountains as we passed them.

Dom whispered quietly in my ear,

'This is where I spend a lot of my time, mum. This is where I'm happy.'

I found myself once more on my walk. The dogs were running along beside me and there were grey clouds above me. I felt in awe of what had just happened and I couldn't stop thanking Dom. I felt as if I had been on the holiday of a lifetime. I felt so rested and ready for the challenges that lay ahead.

My holiday had taken 10 minutes (in our time) but it had rejuvenated me completely. My friend did not need to come and give me a break. Since then I have not looked back. I have also felt very privileged to experience a little of Dom's current reality.

An extra from another source

One morning, I felt the need to sit quietly and, although I was very busy, I knew that I was being urged into a chair in the corner of my kitchen. I therefore obeyed. Immediately, I felt a huge round shadow behind me. My first thought was: 'This is my shadow side.'

I felt very nervous but I never flinched from jumping in to see what there was for me to understand. Once inside, I felt I was engulfed in a grey ball. Further investigation made me realise I was in a graveyard where I saw bodies, bones, old clothes, twigs, roots, fallen trees, barren areas. Nothing was living. The scene I saw depicted physical death from every conceivable walk of life throughout the ages. I tripped up on different bodies that had been occupied by me in various parts of the world, as I travelled over the scene. The lighting was dull and grey and there was a deep feeling of gloom. A quiet voice said to me,

'You are in the graveyard of the world. This is where you all put your families and friends when they die. This is where everything is left to rot. And you do it all with such ceremony and sadness.'

I had a sudden vision of a funeral and a body in a coffin being lowered into the ground. I saw the tears and the prayers and the sadness enter the ground. I saw the people standing crying around the grave and then the earth falling back on top of the coffin. I felt the deep sadness being buried and left.

I realised with horror just how much sadness and death we have all buried and left in the ground. I felt the earth's desperate need to heal. I felt some hidden sadness in my own body and I felt its need to release. I started to ask for my body to lose all the sadness it was carrying from all my lifetimes. Then I asked for the sadness we have all left thoughtlessly in the ground to be freed up so the earth could heal itself. I was truly shocked to feel the extent of 'grey gloom' we have unwittingly planted in our earth. I was indeed seeing a part of my 'shadow' side.

If this experience makes sense to you, I hope you will help release the earth from all you have left in it yourself.

Appendix 2
A Nourishment Diary

During 2010, I had been asking the universe (and Dom) to help me understand what was happening in the world *before* the Split. Little did I know that my first lesson would be so dramatic, and I shall share a little bit of it with you to give you an insight into where this part of my journey is taking me. It starts as a narrative and changes to a diary.

As Dom explained to me during his revelations, the first absorption of nourishment came from the desire of evolving light to aid other evolving light beings to travel independently, while they were seemingly separated from the source.

Nourishment was originally absorbed through the skin as moisture. It was transmitted from one living source (such as grass) to the travelling source (such as the worm), in the belief that this would be the only way the worm could travel without dying. Thus, a state of 'dependency' was created.

From this first 'devouring of each other', a dependency on food has continued to evolve. The first worms and maggots absorbed mostly water but also picked up the essence of the plants, thus merging the two together forever in a new way.

The merging continued because the experiment appeared to work. The worm successfully arrived at its destination and the evolving world began a new era in its development. Creation began to enjoy its merging and so the essences that had developed independently from source, up until that moment, began to lose their purity.

In the excitement of the moment, the merging idea took hold and many other mergers took place very quickly. Hence, all types of new creatures started to evolve and they started to develop means of excretion or, rather, a means of sifting through what they absorbed. Their bodies started to keep what they thought they needed and to discard what they didn't . . .

It had never crossed my mind that one day I would be considering living without food. I ate because I thought I had to. It wasn't something I thought about much, other than that if I ate properly and in a balanced manner I would be healthy and have enough energy for what I wanted to do. I also enjoyed sitting in front of the television with a bar of chocolate or some peanuts on a cold winter's evening. I had never been fussy about food, basically producing for the family the same plain but nourishing fresh diet that my mother had always given me. I had no interest in cooking other than it was something I had to do for the family on a daily basis. Shopping for food had always been a chore but was something that seemed unavoidable and therefore I just got on with it.

I suppose I first became aware of food in a different way when I opened the retreat. I was astonished to find just how many different types of milk there were on the market. For someone who had only ever experienced milk from a cow supplied in milkman-sized bottles (apart from when my son was a baby and was allergic to it so he substituted it with orange juice!), the array of milks that turned up in my fridge was a real eye-opener. I quickly realised I could not cope with this level of diversity so I continued to supply cow's milk in semi-skimmed form for the guests and left it up to them as to whether they used it or not.

I used to supply fine brown bread from the bakers which I felt was suitable for incoming guests but then realised that at least half of them couldn't eat wheat. Couldn't eat wheat? What was this? My brain was struggling to compute!

And, slowly, as more and more guests came to the farm with their weird and wonderful diets, my eyes were opened to the mass of foods (and substitutes) that are available in this country today. Inside, I was always secretly amused at their dietary peculiarities though I never let it show. I witnessed long conversations about food at the farmhouse kitchen table and hardly ever joined in. It just wasn't my scene.

My awakening to the fact that we could exist without food came in quite a roundabout way in the early part of

2010. I was looking through the Cygnus magazines for a book called *Life from Light* (Werner and Stockli, 2007), which I had seen in a previous edition and which I thought I might give to a friend for her birthday, but I couldn't find it. I rang Cygnus and asked if they were still stocking it. They didn't seem to know what I was talking about at the time but in the very next issue of the magazine I noticed the book was advertised. I was amused, realising the universe had probably prompted Cygnus to feature it.

So, I ordered the book . . . and it never reached my friend!

That week I was going on a small holiday for three days and I decided to take the book with me. I think I had only read a few pages when I realised that existing without food was quite possibly a step I was going to take in the future. The author talked about a '21-day process' in which one goes through a three-stage transition in order to start living off light. The stages involve: not eating anything for the first seven days, drinking a little water during the second seven days and drinking a little more water and orange juice during the third seven days. By the time this process is over, he talked about the body having made a complete transition and being able to live permanently off light. I decided then and there to cut out breakfast and see how I felt.

Cutting out breakfast was one of the most dramatic decisions I had made for a while. It wasn't a carefully thought-out decision and because it was done so completely on the spur of the moment, it proved to be a massive learning curve that took me months and months to come to terms with.

As I was on holiday with two friends and we were staying in a hotel that didn't do breakfast, cutting out the meal itself was initially quite easy. What was not so easy was the fact that I had always felt if I didn't eat regularly I would get very weak. This thought consumed me the whole of that first morning, so I asked continually to feed from source (as mentioned in the book I was reading). I was totally surprised to find I did not lose any energy all morning and by lunchtime I was still feeling absolutely fine although very hungry indeed. I wolfed down my lunch with relief and, as I had decided I wouldn't hold back for the rest of the day, I ate anything and everything I wanted.

This pattern continued for the rest of the holiday and I continued to read the book, learning more and more about Michael Werner's journey. By the end of the holiday, I said to my friends,

'I have no idea if I am really going to do this but I am going to go without breakfast for the summer and I may or may not take it further when the retreat closes in October. I know I cannot do it right now. I am still struggling too much after the death of my son, and I am not strong enough, but I may well be strong enough by the autumn.'

And we left it at that.

Coming home and continuing this process was very odd. I lay in bed every morning and asked the universe to sustain me from the light source and trusted that it would happen. I was continually amazed that I never ever ran out of energy though I was always ravenous by lunchtime.

My thoughts at this time were all over the place. Panic, in many ways, set in. I didn't really want to live without my favourite foods for the rest of my life. I suddenly discovered that I really *loved* chocolate after all and I started buying loads of chocolate Easter eggs. (I mean three small ones a week but that was loads for me!) I started buying all the things I loved eating, thinking to myself, 'I've got to eat these now because before long I may not be able to eat them again.'

Food took on a whole new meaning. It suddenly became very important! Very important indeed!

I plodded on with life. I continued to do without breakfast and a mid-morning snack, while eating whatever I wanted during the rest of the day, mostly snacking like billio during the evenings. I never once lost energy! I continued to drink whatever I wanted to at any time.

The most important part of this exercise was that I was training my mind and body to understand that I ate food in the first place and that I may not eat it in the future. For someone who had placed so little importance on food, this was a very big learning curve indeed.

The universe, in its clever way, sent a guest to the retreat who had already been through the '21-day process' (Werner and Stockli, 2007). She seemed very pleased that I understood about her process at all and was more than happy to share her experiences. My youngest son, Edward, and I listened to her while she related her story and we were both very amazed at how easily she spoke about it. I was also very surprised that Edward took such an interest and it became obvious that he too might decide one day to live on light.

Meeting this lady and having her to stay for a week was hugely encouraging to me because I could see at first hand that the journey might be possible for me. It also gave me someone to talk about it with and some experienced support, should I decide to go ahead with the process. I thanked the universe profoundly. A second guest turned up who also claimed to live without eating and I found I didn't need to talk to him at all. I had my inner trust and all the information I required for that moment.

By the autumn, I had grown completely used to not eating until lunchtime. I had got through hay making without any trouble, I had managed the retreat through all its busy periods and I was getting less and less ravenous at lunchtimes. I had never once flagged during the morning and, in fact, I felt very well.

I started to think about the next stage I should go through. My mind had by this time thoroughly got used to the idea that I could live off light. I didn't really want to do it but my instinct told me it was the next step in my ascension process and it could be very helpful. It felt as if the universe had definitely pointed me in this direction because it was something I needed to do in order to become 'lighter' and to enhance my connection to source.

By this time, my body was starting to feel uncomfortable if it had lots of food in it. I was aware of excreting food as soon as possible because I didn't like the feeling of being full. I became increasingly aware of the lack of necessity of the whole digestive process.

I began thinking seriously about what I should do. I read a book, *Living on Light,* written by Jasmuheen, who had undergone the 21-day process in 1993 and is now an expert on the subject (Jasmuheen, 1998). She described the process she went through in detail and how it impacted on her then and now. I was making plans. I told my son I was going to do the 21-day process just after Christmas when our family and guests had gone. I asked him if he would look after me. I felt very daunted by the whole thing and yet was feeling an increasing determination to go through with it. I decided to cut out all the snacks I was having in the evenings as my next preparation.

I read through the 21-day process again. I was uncomfortable. Something wasn't sitting right. Did I really need to go through this process? Couldn't I just gradually cut out food? Did I really have to go through this major trauma? I felt I had had enough traumas in my life and it wasn't making sense to go through another.

I thought seriously about the revelations that I had received. I thought about the journey the first worms had made from one tree to another. I remembered how the grass had called out to the worms: 'Eat me! Absorb me! I will help you make the journey.'

I felt strongly that we didn't really need to eat, not because we could live off light but because we had initially started eating because we thought we were separated from source when we left that first tree. It was an illusion. We are source! We don't need to absorb each other to survive. We don't need to eat each other. We just ARE!

The next day, I was due to go for a day-long walk with some friends. Strangely I didn't have an opportunity to eat anything until 4.30 p.m. that day. I did not run out of energy and I felt a little hungry but otherwise not too bad. I kept telling myself: 'Eating is a habit! You know perfectly well you don't need to eat.' In fact, I didn't have a proper meal that day at all and went to bed feeling very light.

The following morning, I was due to play a tennis match at 10.00 a.m. During the first few games of the first set, I suddenly realised it was the first time I had ever done anything competitive without eating breakfast. I then panicked when I remembered I had not eaten much at all the day before. I told myself quietly: 'It's OK. Eating is an illusion. You don't need food.'

I asked for help from the universe and, almost immediately, I started to play tennis in an incredible way. I could suddenly hit the ball strongly and beautifully. My reactions were so fast and I had plenty of energy. I felt fantastic. After a first very tight, very demanding set, I started to wobble. I thought: 'I can't do this again!'

And the second set was full of an internal argument with myself as to whether I could or couldn't do it again. I still played very well but the internal argument took the edge off things. I began to feel light-headed and a little as if I couldn't see clearly, so I said to the universe: 'Please help me have the energy I need to do this.' Straight away I felt better and my vision cleared.

I WAS BEING FULLY SUPPORTED!!!

After that set, I succumbed to the pressure and ate four Jaffa cakes (basically the only food to hand!) I then played a further two sets with no trouble at all, playing the best tennis I could ever remember.

All the way home, I didn't feel hungry. I was really quite stunned. Could my tennis have been affected by my increasing dependence on the universe to sustain me? I had been so quick. My reactions had been so improved. I felt so good! I felt so clear!

That evening, I started to suspect that I may not need to go through the 21-day process at all. I was starting to feel as if my body already knew all it needed to know and that it was going to be a simple process of gradually cutting down on my food intake and clearing myself totally of the illusion that I needed to eat in order to survive.

Living off light? I *am* the light.

My Food Diary

Monday 22 November 2010

I've made a decision! I'm going to stay with just the two meals a day for a little while. Then, I'm going to cut it down to one. Then, if I haven't cut it all out by Christmas, I will go ahead and finish it off with my own version of the 21-day process. I don't intend to give up drink yet, if ever! I can't see the need. This is not about 'proving' that one can live off light for me, for I already know that I can. I think this is about becoming lighter or getting clearer and nearer to oneness.

I'm now living very much from moment to moment. I am not trying to put exact timings on things, as just the outline above is enough. Taking one day at a time is much less worrying for me.

I do hate the way this process is so all-consuming but I can't see any way around it. We are so programmed to eat. It is such a very hard habit to stop!

Thursday 25 November

I am now getting quite used to only eating twice a day and not snacking at all. I am starting to eat lighter and less and my energy is so far quite high. In fact, I feel really well with no weight loss that I can tell (as in my trousers fit around my waist in the same way).

I went shopping today. I waved at the foods that I normally buy and said 'hello' and 'thank you' to them.

I seem to be going long hours without eating, quite successfully and not even feeling hungry when it is my allotted time to eat. But I do feel the need to tread carefully and to do this little by little and with the least possible fuss.

Friday 26 November

I ate some chocolate yesterday evening. It was really interesting because when I got into bed I felt uncomfortable and could actually feel the chocolate sitting heavily inside me. I mustn't do that again. I didn't feel right again until lunchtime today when my energy shot up again. When I went for a walk this afternoon, I got up the hills very easily. Normally it's quite a struggle and I'm used to a struggle. It felt odd to shoot up the hill without the struggle! It seems the less I eat the better my energy levels are.

I'm just eating very light food now and not very much compared with what I was eating! I'm drinking whenever I want to though.

Monday 29 November

I have been feeling uneasy about things. I'm not keen to do the 21-day process at all. I've been wavering on and off about the whole thing in general. Do I really need to do this?

I had the idea of looking at Jasmuheen's website (www.jasmuheen.com). The book I have been reading about her was written during the 1990s (Jasmuheen, 1998). How does she feel about things now? Wow! On the website, it confirms everything I have been thinking. Gosh! She has changed! All the things I have been intuitively doing are now in her eyes the correct things to do. She no longer talks about the 21-day process. She talks about doing this thing gradually! Nearly everything she says on her website confirms my intuitive thoughts. It's like a huge weight off my mind.

Right! I will stay with this process and see where it leads me. I can see now that by continually asking source to be 'clearer', the only road that I *could* take is this one! There's not a lot else major to clear! But what I have been filling my body with, although it's not outwardly harming me, is holding up my spiritual progress.

So, I pray now that I take this process at the right pace and in the right way for my own highest good. All will be well.

Wednesday 8 December

In the last few days, I have been rebelling against the whole idea of 'not eating' and I have been asking for help.

I haven't felt too good in my tummy because of putting some heavier foods in it so yesterday I ate salad and felt much better. I woke this morning feeling in good balance and that all was right with the world again. I had to take my car into the garage for a service and as I drove onto the forecourt I hit a post that was frozen into the ground. I hit it gently, I was driving very slowly and I damaged the middle section of one side of my car. I will have to have a new door and a new side panel. 'Why', I asked myself, 'why would I do that, when I feel so in balance?'

It didn't take me long to realise that the universe had found a clever way of showing me the damage I am doing to myself when I eat. I'm damaging my tummy section, gently, nothing serious and there is no one else involved. But the degree of damage to my car is proportionate to the damage I am doing to my tummy. I thought about my car. Wow! It needed a new door and a new side panel. It was exterior work and nothing serious, but expensive to put right and *more damage than I could possibly have believed for such a small incident.* So, I must be doing more damage to my own vehicle (my body) than I had realised, by eating!

Well, I asked for help and I've got it. I will remember the damage to my car for a long while because it is so costly, so I will not forget the unnecessary damage I am doing to my body now.

I've had another thought. As I *know* I do not need food now, is the damage done by eating increased now? In other words, food didn't damage me in the past because I didn't know I shouldn't eat it but now I know food is superfluous, is it more damaging? Possibly. Right! I'd better get my car fixed and I'd better fix myself too.

Thursday 9 December

The new regime has started. I don't drink hot chocolate any more and I am tuning in to the foods that I am eating carefully to see if they feel right, and I am eating slightly less than I was during the two meals that I do have. I've cut out a lot of hot Ribena drinks and I am having hot water instead.

I feel quite hungry tonight but I know it's only habit. Food is *such* a habit. My energy is the same as usual, not more, not less. My weight feels stable.

Sunday 12 December

I have been feeling hungry so I decided to eat a little more. I'm back to two proper meals a day. I feel tired and I have a cold so that could be throwing things a bit. I think I will stabilise like this for a few days and then see how I'm led.

Thursday 16 December

I am so confused. I'm still basically sticking to two meals a day but feeling I should give up meat as it doesn't do me much good. Well, it's OK, but I feel I am eating animals' energy and this is affecting my own purity. I think I might go back to going through the 21-day process after all. I might do it very soon in the New Year but get Christmas over first. Not sure.

Saturday 18 December

This morning I discovered something shocking. I have a cyst on my back which has gradually been getting bigger and sorer during the last week. I tried tuning in again to see if I could understand why it is there. What *is* it that I *will not* face? I have been trying so desperately to know, all week.

Suddenly, I saw maggots and worm-like creatures spilling out of the cyst. To say I was shocked is an understatement. I was devastated. My cyst was showing me I had been a maggoty, worm-like creature that had been one of the first parts of the 'light' to eat! I had been one of the creatures trying to make the journey from one tree to another (so to speak) and I had been one of the first to absorb others!

The guilt I felt at that moment was astronomic. I knew it was true. I recognised that energy within myself. I knew I had been a pioneer at that time, at the forefront of the light forcing outwards from source. I could feel the competitiveness within myself, wanting to be one of the first to make the journey. So I had listened to the call from my fellow beings: 'Eat me, absorb me. We will help you survive the journey.'

And I 'absorbed'. Yes, I absorbed. In that moment, I helped to create a fresh type of dependency. I moved creation further from source towards thinking we needed to absorb each other to survive.

I lay in bed, sadly taking in my part of the responsibility for that moment. It didn't matter to me that millions of others alive today are also responsible. I took on *my* part of the responsibility, in its entirety. I suddenly understood why I was being shown I could take the path of 'not eating' if I chose. For if I decided to do so, I could rectify the 'me' that had chosen to eat so long ago. I could reverse my personal part of that unnecessary energy and would therefore be bringing that part of the 'light' back to the planet.

Not only would I be helping the planet in this way, I would also be doing it from a place of plenty. I live in a country where food is overflowing, where every type of food is accessible at almost any time of year. My fridge is full of all I could wish for. I can eat whatever I want when I want.

But, if I choose to turn away from it, if I choose to proceed with the 21-day process, or if I choose to prove I can survive without food, I *will* reverse the damage done so long ago and in the highest possible way.

So, now I have a true purpose. Isn't this what I was asking for? Help? And I now have that help. I *will* do it. I *have* to. I need to live a life where I can truly 'be' in a place where I have no food dependency. It doesn't matter what happens afterwards. I just need to 'do' it. I need to put right my bit of the process. My fight is over!

I also now know that this diary needs to be a part of my next book. It's no good hiding. I've done that before and it almost killed me. So blow. And blow again! I'm going to have to let it be known.

Sunday 26 December

I can't start the 21-day process yet. I now have cysts popping up all over my body and I have a lump under my arm. The doctor has just put me on antibiotics—he says my system is being poisoned by something and he is trying to reduce the inflammation in the cysts. It's all quite scary. I rang Jasmuheen (who had become my mentor) today and she said not to start until I am off the antibiotics and well on the mend. I need to try and find out why the cysts don't seem to be disappearing. Also, what is going on under my arm?

Anyway, I've taken myself off all animal and dairy products because, instinctively, I feel they may be contributing to my cysts. It seems as though I am letting toxins out or trying to. I have toothache today too. Something else is brewing.

Wednesday 29 December

A vegetable box arrived in the post today: a mass of vegetables from an old friend of Dom's who knows nothing about what is going on with me. In fact, he hardly knows me at all! I am staggered. Why should he suddenly decide to send me vegetables? It's crazy.

This must be a massive sign from the universe that it's OK for me to eat vegetables. And vegetables of all descriptions! I've never seen so many different varieties. Right! I'm tucking in!

Friday 31 December

After a perfectly ghastly few days and after much advice from nutritionists and Jasmuheen herself, I have decided my cysts, and now an abscess behind my tooth, are not getting better because I am trying to detoxify too fast. In purifying my diet so quickly (have been down to only vegetables and rice today), I am pushing my cells into letting too many toxins into the blood stream and my liver can't cope.

So, it seems that slow and steady is the rule of thumb. I was only panicking because I thought that if I don't do it now, I won't have time again this year because of opening the retreat again in April. But what does it matter if I do or don't do it now? The most important thing is that I have the intention and also that I believe, 100 per cent, that I *can* live off light. What has happened through this though is that I will be eating a much cleaner and more organic diet from now on.

The experts no longer advocate doing the 21-day process. They say it only has a 10 per cent success rate and has proved too shocking for the body. They now advocate listening to your intuition and doing it slowly . . . So, I've gone full circle.

OK, I am currently on two types of antibiotic, one from the doctor and one from the dentist, and facing a small operation on Tuesday to remove the cysts. I shall get that done first and see what happens after that.

Saturday 1 January 2011

As I went to sleep last night, I asked the universe if there was anything further I needed to understand at this point. Then this morning I awoke to 'further understandings'! During the Christmas period, when I was enduring all the pain, I lost my way somewhat. I forgot that this process is all about 'cleansing' and it became a mad dash for 'clearing the poisons from my body so I could get out of pain'. This morning, having calmed myself yesterday, I was able to receive the reality of the situation.

Coming off dairy and meat was entirely right. Coming off sugars at this point was not as necessary as I had first supposed. Understanding what different foods do to the body has been invaluable; starting a cleansing process of all the products in my house has been very helpful. I remembered that in the autumn I had been asking that my everyday internal clearing process should not be so laborious. I had also constantly been asking to clear myself further from unkind thoughts. In fact, I had at one point got so cross with myself for thinking (bad) thoughts that I had said very firmly: 'No! I won't have this any more. It's not who I want to be. Please, please help me stop this!'

I realise now that the cyst on my back started to grow at this point and it was indeed coinciding with the cutting down of snacks which, of course, meant I was taking in fewer harmful products. My body started to react and my liver started to be overloaded with the toxins trying to escape, so cysts and other eliminations started to appear through my skin.

When I cut out dairy and meat on Boxing Day, I must have been overloading my liver again and so the cysts couldn't recover as they were still needed as exit points. My poor body! It's been trying to clear itself of animal energies and I've been fighting the clearing process! So I have now asked the universe to help my liver to cope and to allow the drainage of the toxins to come out in the normal way so my skin can recover. I am well into the main part of eliminating the toxins, so it should be OK.

I have now understood that I have had to undergo an increasingly laborious 'cleansing of energy' process on a several-times-a-day basis, because I was choosing to ingest animal energies. If I now went back to eating meat, I would have to do this again, in order to maintain the level of clarity I have grown used to. If I choose *not* to eat animals, I will not need to laboriously clear myself from their energies. It's my choice! This will also apply to sugars, vegetables and anything else that I choose to eliminate from my system, at some later stage, should I decide to continue this process and cleanse further. But, next time, I will understand the process and will do it more calmly, slowly and gently so my body can cope.

I have noticed that, on several occasions in the last few weeks, my spontaneous reactions to certain situations have improved and I have been surprised and very pleased. Now I know why.

Of course, my choice is that I do not wish to ingest animal energy again. I know if it happens by accident it doesn't matter at all. I will simply ask to clear my body of the offending energies.

Sunday 2 January

I am trying not to fight what I *have* to do. My whole self wants to go back to eating and drinking my old diet. I yearn for what I am used to, food that I know, normality. If I had a choice, I would eat what I have always eaten and just die when my number is up. This whole process, for me, is torture.

As I lay in the bath, I pondered my misery. I fully allowed the emotion to swamp me and then I started to remember countless past lives in which I had died from starvation. I was amazed and yet not amazed. But I now understood my paralysing fear . . .

Later that day, I sat eating my vegetable supper in complete misery. I asked for help. My whole body screamed for help. And, of course, help came.

Our whole purpose on this planet is to 'consciously' return to the level of light that exists at source. Our current major step is to bring back the light as it was before the Split. The actual moment of rebalancing is fast approaching. I can feel an urgency that is unrelenting. There is no more time to waste. There are humans incarnate now who are working unbelievably hard to bring the rebalance about. I am one of those humans, but there are others doing better than me. If I achieve reaching the level of light that we had before the Split, I am bringing that level of light *voluntarily* into consciousness. My sacrifice is not just a selfish one. By living in one of the most affluent countries in the world, where any food I want is at my fingertips, and voluntarily giving the tastiest bits up, I am taking myself back to the level of light before the Split. On a personal level, I am making up for my past and on a world level, I am enabling the light to come through me at the level the planet needs right now.

Slowly my cysts continue to improve. Slowly the toxins are eliminating themselves. Slowly I will take these last steps as guided and needed . . .

Thursday 6 January

All is on course. My skin continues to improve. My state of mind is rebalancing. My body is getting used to its new regime. I am healing . . . I will let the future take care of itself!

Sunday 9 January

I cannot describe adequately in words what is going on now. I just know that I am daily becoming an increasingly effective channel for the level of light that existed on earth before the Split. Joy, peace, love and wisdom are coming back into balance deep within me.

I have *yearned* for this moment. I have yearned to reconnect with this level of light. I know I have still so much to learn but I have cleared myself enough at this point in time to feel the benefits of all my past efforts and to know they have been worthwhile. I represent, in my own small way, the truth of all I have searched for.

Tuesday 15 March

I had completely decided that whatever 'odd' things I was going through with my diet, I would never impose my situation on anyone else. So when my 86-year-old godmother invited me for lunch and cooked a chicken dish, I simply thought to myself that it is in the highest interests not to upset her and to appreciate her meal so I will eat it. I thoroughly enjoyed it, even though I had not eaten meat for two and a half months. We both had a very enjoyable day.

That evening, however, I felt rather unwell with a stomach ache. I felt the meat sitting heavily inside me. I knew I didn't have a bug although I felt sick. I felt unwell all that night and into the next morning. My whole body balance felt rocky. I desperately wanted the meat out of my system. During that day, of course, it passed through and

I began to feel better. However, the difficulty was that I had been invited out to lunch the following day. I knew I couldn't go through this again, so what to do?

I emailed my friends and told them what had happened and they emailed back to say everything was absolutely fine and I could eat what I wanted. They thanked me for telling them in advance. I relaxed and felt even better. So, the conclusion I have come to this morning is that I must inform people and risk making a 'nuisance' of myself after all! I now realise that my stomach can actually no longer tolerate meat. I have changed that much, that quickly. I am going to have to become the 'pain in the neck' I have never wanted to be.

Tuesday 5 April

I maintain the 'breakfast' regime because it helps me bring to mind the fact that we don't 'need' to eat, every day. Also, if I deviate from my current diet in any way, I suffer for it so I know I am doing the right thing for now. When we have gone through the 'shift', I know that further progress towards 'living off light' will become much easier . . . I am at peace.

Tuesday 3 May

This morning, I understand that one day I really will live without eating. I don't have to worry about when, I don't need to force the issue, I don't need to starve. I don't even know if it will be during this lifetime! I simply need to let go and be guided through the process. It will happen as it happens. I do need to listen to instincts such as: don't be greedy, don't eat animal, enjoy what is before you, be thankful for what is before you and available to you, etc. I do need to be ready to hear further moves . . . as and when!

Bigger than this is the realisation that this process goes far beyond food. I have let go (to as deep a level as I can) of as many barriers as I am able, such as the need for: electricity, warmth, clothing, a safe place to live, friends, family, fuel, money, a car, etc. Somehow all of this 'attachment' will be unnecessary soon and the 'being condition' we are searching for will just 'be there'. How we get there will soon unfold. Plants will re-educate and only grow where they are required and not stifle their compatriots. Poisonous plants will no longer be able to kill. Foxes will no longer wish to eat my hens and the hens will be able to run free safely. I will no longer need field fences.

I do not have to force this issue in any way. It is enough to understand it and trust the process as deeply as I can. In the greater understanding of these possibilities, I am bringing the belief into consciousness and that is enough for now. I must allow myself to be intuitively led. I must trust this conscious process.

Monday 5 June

I have already realised I have died from starvation in many lifetimes and have asked to be healed from all the hurt those experiences left me with but I still haven't made much progress on that level.

This morning, I came to realise that the fear I experienced on my initial separation from the bulk of the light, plays a part in causing me to eat. It gives me a link I subconsciously think I need and so I am now asking to be healed from all the terror related to that moment. I believe this terror impacts on me in many other ways too.

Monday 1 August

I'm still eating much the same foods. However, I no longer turn to food when I am emotionally upset. I think of turning to it, but that thought comes less and less. I now enjoy what I eat and appreciate it as never before. I eat much less so it has become something I look forward to instead of experiencing eating as a nuisance. I know deep down that I do not need to eat anything but if I try and eat less, at the moment, I still become very hungry. Therefore, I don't fight it because I believe I am retraining my eating habit slowly and there will be a time in the future to reduce my eating. I suppose you could say I am growing into my new regime and accepting it in the now.

Saturday 3 September

For the last few weeks, I have been questioning why I am so obsessed with getting to lunchtime every day so I can eat. I haven't given in and eaten but I am always so thankful to reach lunchtime at which time I eat plenty, knowing

I can't eat again until the evening. These thoughts didn't worry me until recently because I thought they would just go away but now I have had to acknowledge I am rather stuck! So, I have been asking for help!

Last night, I had the most peculiar diarrhoea. It kept rumbling away in my intestine and only came out in very tiny amounts. It didn't seem like a tummy bug and I certainly felt very well. This continued all night so I kept asking for a reason. Then I fell asleep and dreamt I was in Peru, in very ancient days. I knew they were ancient because I kept seeing myself fall through the earth from today's existence to an existence well below the earth's surface. I dreamt this same dream three times. It was as far as the dream went.

In the morning, my tummy was exactly the same but I felt really well so I decided to look into my rumbling intestine to see what was going on. I became aware of myself as a very early human. I was travelling along on my knees and elbows, scuffling my face, nose and mouth into the dirty, sandy soil. The soil was grey and very dry. I could feel my mouth searching for things to eat and I picked up a charred stick with my lips and ate it. I continued on and found a dry piece of reed and ate that. There really wasn't much food around. The interesting thing was that I didn't look for food with my eyes but I felt for it with my face and mouth, taking in quite a bit of dirt as I did so. A little after that, I felt a piece of lush grass on my lips and I quickly pressed my whole face and mouth into it in a ravenous way. I tore at its roots rapidly using my teeth and felt its goodness go into my stomach. The experience was so real that I felt as if I was doing it at that very moment. The feeling of deliciousness on finding the soft luscious grass was extreme and I felt rewarded for all my hard work in my search for sustenance.

Then I felt a soft worm near my lips. I acknowledged my fellow friend and allowed it to eat all that I was eating. I shared unconditionally and the worm was my equal. There was nothing in me that wished to eat the worm. The thought didn't even cross my mind. He was a fellow creature, 'making his journey' as I was.

I came up off my elbows at one point and excreted from my rear end just where I was. I didn't stay upright longer than was necessary, and afterwards simply resumed my search for food.

I never seemed to use my hands. I knew they were there but they didn't come into this picture. They seemed to hang like useless extras as I moved. Sometimes I could feel my back end rise onto my feet but my elbows didn't seem to leave the ground. I was on a mission for food in order to get from 'a' to 'b' and there was nothing but survival in my head.

I smelt water in the distance. I went to the water and it was filthy, muddy and full of insects. I drank deeply without a care.

I sat and marvelled at this scene. I feel I have re-experienced a very early human state that was little different to that of an animal. I felt akin to one of my Dartmoor ponies who rip relentlessly at the green grass after I have let them out of their starvation paddock.

I know this is just a link in the chain of what I have to understand but I am very grateful to have had this memory as I deepen my journey back in time.

Sunday 6 November

On my trip to Peru, I had to eat a few things I wouldn't normally eat. Walking at high altitude wasn't easy and I found I needed a greater sugar intake. However, I didn't let it worry me. I just ate what I needed to. I also had to eat fish or cheese occasionally as there was nothing else.

Now I am back in England, I have gone back to my former regime. I believe that cutting out animal products from my diet is all that is required of me at present. It has certainly made me feel clearer and free from any unwanted emotions that animal products had previously given me. I am currently very healthy, despite having lost a fair bit of weight. I suspect I may well do some individual fasting days this winter. Hunger is slowly becoming less of a problem to me. My dependence on food is gradually diminishing. I do not regret anything I am doing for I feel very comfortable within. One day, as guided, I may yet 'live off light'.

My Food Diary

I hope that having shared my 'nourishment' journey, as it currently stands, has been helpful to you. Everyone has to experience things in their own way. If I had my time again, I would not have cut so many things out of my diet so quickly. I believe that contributed to all the cysts and made my body go into shock. Anything I do in the future will be done more gently.

Now, 18 months on from the start of my journey, I know that because I am *willing* to undergo 'living off light' as required at every level, I have overcome the 'dependency' I helped to create in the first place.

I wish you all the best on your own nutritional journey.

References

BBC (2011a) *The Frozen Planet.* London: BBC.

BBC (2011b) *The Wonders of the Universe.* London: BBC.

Delves, A. (2008) *From Chrysalis to Butterfly.* London: AuthorHouse.

Jasmuheen (1998) *Living on Light: The Source of Nourishment for the New Millennium.* Burgrain, Germany: Koha Publishing.

Werner, M. and Stockli, T. (2007) *Life from Light: Is it Possible to Live Without Food?* Forest Row: Clairview Books.

Lightning Source UK Ltd.
Milton Keynes UK
UKHW010507090519
342370UK00001B/5/P